THE SPIRITUALITY OF THE SACRAMENTS

THE SPIRITUALITY
OF THE SACRAMENTS

Doctrine and Practice for Today

by BERNARD BRO, O.P.

translated by Theodore DuBois

SHEED AND WARD: NEW YORK

Contents

THE SPIRITUALITY OF THE SACRAMENTS

Introduction:
Questions of a Practicing Christian

If there is a God, how can we stand not being Him?

NIETZSCHE

God's love for man is that God has made Himself its proof.

AL HALLAJ

The one who built you will wed you.

IS. 62:5

The Word of God became man so that man can become God. He became visible in his body so that he could give us an idea of the invisible Father. He bore the outrages of men so that we could share in immortality.

ST. ATHANASIUS

When death was what they deserved, you have given them time and room to rid themselves of wickedness.

WIS. 12:20

Before your eyes Jesus Christ was portrayed as crucified.

GAL. 3:1

Two men sixty years old, both belong to the same religious Order. Their positions in the Church lead us to believe that their lives are a "success"; they can look behind them. And this is what they do.

All at once, because they went through the novitiate together, they ask each other why they entered the Order, why one gave up a career in law and the other a career of university research.

They finally come up with only one reason, and each, as he protests that he is not being sentimental, admits that he entered religion because if he had stayed in the world, he would have felt that he was committing a kind of suicide. And they conclude by asking themselves how entrance into religion can be a question of life or death.

Rainer Maria Rilke answered a young poet who had sent him a few poems and asked for his opinion on them, "Would you die if you were forbidden to write? If yes, then continue; if not, then it is useless."

As he listened to his two elders, the author of this book understood better just how far Christ wanted to enter his life. In writing the pages that follow, he often tried to make the reasons for this love of Christ objective and communicable. But beyond these reasons, as far back as he can remember, he knows that he has always needed Christ to live.

It is necessary to be pure to approach God. Does this mean, then, not having any more problems? And what is to be done about those who have unsolvable problems? Wouldn't membership in the Church then be reserved to mild temperaments or great virtue?

The Gospel is addressed to everyone. But aren't the liturgy and the sacraments addressed only to those who have the time, the culture, and the possibility to understand a language of initiates?

Why is it so difficult to see the relationship which the sacraments have with our life? For example, why is it that sometimes when we come out of the confessional we have the impression that we have said nothing, or said nothing essential? We use words that are clichés, and the catalogues of sins betray our desire to be true. How can the word "impurity" have the same meaning for everyone?

Isn't it our liberty, our spontaneous adhesion, our love which counts most in face of God? Don't we therefore feel some kind of artificial constraint in the sacraments? Are we being sincere when we follow the rhythms of a practice that is composed from the exterior?

Because they constantly place intermediaries, things to do, and rites to practice, between God and ourselves, don't the sacraments cause us to lose the sense of God's personal intervention in our life?

If God is in us, why do we need a presence in the Eucharist? But if Christ is "really" present, why do we think about it and imagine it so little? If there is not a real presence, if it is not Christ, then what good is everything else?

Aren't the sacraments an additional occasion for us to avoid the real questions and to content ourselves with the *status quo?* When they simply set us right with the obligations of our parish, family, or community, aren't the sacraments allowing us to get off easily with our conscience?

We need to be honest in discovering our limitations and our frailty in face of hard and difficult things; but in view of the sometimes artificial appearance of the sacraments, aren't we tempted to consider them facile tranquilizers for deficient souls?

Doesn't the Gospel speak first of all of poverty and charity, whereas the liturgy speaks of richness, ritual, and obligations? Why doesn't it appear more clearly that receiving the sacraments leads to a greater charity?

Even if we give a greater role to the laity because we must make concessions to the modern world, doesn't the *a priori* obedience which the Church expects in the sacraments cause us to retain a childish attitude? Isn't the fact that many persons stop practicing their religion after the age of twelve due to their search elsewhere for true responsibilities which can enable them to develop?

When we go to Confession, how can we place ourselves between mercy and justice, without weakening one by the other? God is just, but not too much, because he is merciful. God is merciful, but we must not trust too much in his mercy, because he is nevertheless just. If God, then, has two faces, which one concerns us?

Should we go to Confession as a necessary routine to keep our soul healthy, or because of a personal discipline we have acquired, or because everyone does it on the eves of holy days? Or should we wait for real repentance born from encounter with Christ? In the latter case, aren't we risking a rather long wait?

Isn't it lying to keep repeating things that we will almost certainly begin again?

How can we know our sins if there are not laws to guide us; but how can we love laws? What we need is the face of Christ, but where can we find it?

And what trust can we have when what was mortal sin yesterday, is no longer so today: for example, the young woman in difficulty who looks for help to a priest but hears him answer, "I do not know what to tell you; in my day, when I learned Canon Law, it was considered to be a sin . . . but we are not sure anymore."

When the prodigal son returned to his father, the latter did not ask him what he had done. He had found his child. What good does it do to recount failings and to delay on them if God already knows them?

Why do we find a tendency in the modern liturgy to suppress the times of silence and to be afraid of them, whereas modern psychologists are discovering the necessity of silence for everyone?

Why does the Church always seem to fear things being really things? For example, at Baptism, why do we always find ourselves using "little" pieces of cotton, a "little" bit of salt, a "little" bit of water, "little" vials of chrism and oil, an old candle . . . , whereas we are actually sharing the illumination, the flavor, and the hospitality of God? Why is it so necessary that at Mass everything be explained to us, whereas, in principle, everything should be clear? Why do we receive Confirmation so early? Shouldn't there then be an eighth sacrament to ratify our commitment in adult life?

Why does the ordination of priests involve such long ceremonies and a constant reminding of the community that it has a role to play and that priests are ordained for the community, if, in fact, we allow the community nothing to say?

Why have we kept the same formula for all marriages for so

long? For those who are prepared, and for those who are not prepared; for those who are young, and for those who are older; for those who look at marriage as a remedy and count on it for their fidelity, and for those who do not?

CAN WE DO WITHOUT THE SACRAMENTS?

In one of his sermons, St. Augustine mentions his surprise that the Good Thief understood the Bible better than the doctors of Israel. He asks whether he perhaps had studied the Scriptures between his acts of plundering. How had he been able to penetrate the meaning of Isaiah 53 whose fulfillment the doctors of the Law had not been able to recognize even when on Calvary it was occurring before their very eyes and by their own efforts? How did it happen that the Good Thief chose as his time to confess the divinity of Christ the very moment when the disciples no longer believed in it?

Then the author puts the following answer into the mouth of the Good Thief: "No, I had not studied the Scriptures, but Jesus looked at me, and in his look I understood everything."

So long as we have not somehow understood everything even before it is explained to us, we have understood nothing in Christianity. Like the Good Thief, every one of us must one day understand that God is really there and that he invites us. We must discover that our answer to his call will be our happiness, and primarily that it will be his glory.

And this invitation and our answer are accomplished in the sacraments. Above and beyond everything which this book can say about the mystery of the sacraments, we must not forget the essential which is this glance of Christ, this encounter between Christ and each one of us, an encounter which converts us and saves us, as it did the Good Thief, and outside of which we can understand nothing.

To better measure the gravity, the stakes, and the place of the sacraments in our life, we will cite here a little illustration. In the last century, one of the philosopher-theologians who best thought out and expressed the sense which Christ's death and resurrection have for us, explained the destiny of the Christian in a parable. In his *Journal* of 1855 Kierkegaard entitled it, "The White Point on the Horizon."

Imagine a very large ship, still larger than our greatest modern ships; it can transport thousands of passengers, and, of course, everything is arranged with the greatest possible comfort, and luxury. It is towards evening. People are enjoying themselves in the parlors; everything is brilliant under the sumptuous lighting; they are listening to a concert. In short, there is only joy, merry-making, and enjoyment; and the noise of this unleashed gaiety echoes through the night air.

The captain is standing on the bridge; and next to him the second-officer takes his binoculars from his eyes and hands them to the captain who answers, "No need, I can see well enough the little white point on the horizon: the night will be terrible."

And then, with the noble and resolute calmness of an experienced sailor, he gives out his orders: "All hands will be on the alert tonight; and I myself will take command."

He goes to his room to wait. He does not have many books, but he has a Bible. He opens it, and strangely enough his eyes fall on the passage, "This very night, your soul will be asked of you." Really strange!

After recollecting himself in meditation and prayer, he dresses for the night-watch; and now, alert and ready for his job, he is the sailor of experience.

In the parlor, the amusement goes on. We can hear the music and the songs, conversation and tumult, the clatter of dishes and plates, the popping of champagne corks; the captain's health is toasted, etc. "The night will be terrible. And perhaps, this very night, your soul will be demanded of you."

Isn't it terrible? And yet, I know something that is still more terrible.

The situation is the same; but the captain is a different person. People are amusing themselves in the parlor, and the gayest of all is the captain.

The white point on the horizon is there, and the night will be terrible. But no one sees the white point or suspects what it forewarns. But no (and this makes it all the more terrible), no, there is one who sees it and who knows what it forewarns. He has no command over the ship; he can take charge of nothing. But, in order not to leave undone anything within his power, he asks the captain to come up onto the bridge, even for only an instant. The captain makes him wait; then he finally comes, but he doesn't want to hear anything and he quickly goes back down to the parlor to share in the noisy and disorderly joy of the passengers who drink to his health and to whom he addresses his warm thanks.

In the agony of his worry, the poor passenger decides to trouble the captain once again; and this time the captain treats him quite impolitely. Nevertheless, the white point remains the same on the horizon: "The night will be terrible."

Isn't this still more terrible? It is terrible to see these thousands of unworried and noisy passengers; terrible to see that the captain is the only one to know what is going to happen; but the essential thing is that he knows it. And it is still more terrible, therefore, that the only one to see and to know the imminent peril should be a passenger.

This is the way in which Kierkegaard tries to picture

Christ on the sea of darkness, in hope that men will feel his presence and take account of the importance of what is at stake. The Christian is this passenger, this single conscious passenger. The luminous point is Christ's approach, his entrance into our lives. Kierkegaard stretches the picture according to his tragic temperament.

Even though this little story is not talking about the sacraments and we can find other applications for it, it nevertheless remains difficult to find another illustration so well suited to show us how we can remain indifferent in face of the mystery of death and resurrection continually occurring for us in the encounter with Someone—Christ. We sometimes forget that this encounter is at the center of our life and that we cannot remain insensitive to it.

Proceeding from this, we can ask: if the sacraments are the means which the Church gives us for our salvation, how do they help us to pass from death to life? What do they have to do with the encounter with Christ? Must we not go beyond them? Must we still receive the sacraments? Or can we dispense with them?

Whether we want to admit it or not, it is perhaps more difficult to have faith today. There are many signs which substantiate this; weariness, loss of a certain sense of life, the wearing away of the greater exigencies with regard to chastity for example, lack of respect for life, a great weakening of the sense of truth, etc. We might answer that all this is quite normal, and demonstrate the contrary by pointing to the renewal of faith due to these very difficulties.

Nevertheless, we cannot deny that it is becoming more difficult to practice our religion because use of the sacraments is posing questions for everyone.

There are certainly many ways of *avoiding questions* which

trouble us: we can refuse to listen to them, we can act as though they concern only other people, we can replace them with other easier questions, or we can pretend that we already know the answers. Regarding the questions posed by the sacraments, we must admit that we do quite well at calling on one of these alibis or another.

And quite often, *we avoid the question*. One of our history books in talking about the French Revolution, mentions an anecdote of those times. In 1787, just before the Constituent Assembly, the Minister of Finances, Calonne, dressed like a head-cook, called together the notables, pictured as fowl, and told them, "I have called you together to know what sauce you want to be eaten in." When the unfortunates tried to make him understand that they did not want to be eaten at all, the minister answered, "Sirs, you are avoiding the question." We Christians can transpose this anecdote: we are all questioned. And we are free. "We do not want to be eaten at all. . . . You are avoiding the question." For us, it is a much greater matter. It concerns what is to decide our life. It concerns knowing whether, like the Good Thief, we accept this encounter. It concerns losing ourselves in order to be assimilated by God, finally offering everything, as God proposes to us in an intervention so hidden and so modest, the intervention of the sacraments, that we constantly risk avoiding the real question.

We can dispense with the sacraments. The wearing of time, fatigue and negligence quickly give rise to alibis. We can practice merely to put ourselves in order or because of social propriety. Or again, more nobly, our ambition to live a more generous or more spiritual life can bring us to relegate the sacraments to second place, after Catholic Action or the apostolate. Simple routine (even for a priest, the fact of carrying out every day a sublime act) becomes a trying task. We find it difficult to take seriously acts that are so simple and humble in comparison with the destiny of man, just as Naaman the Syrian hesitated to plunge into the Jordan because this act seemed to him too simple to cure him of his leprosy (II Kings 5).

We are still faced with the question: as far as we may penetrate into the depths of Christianity (with regard to the life of prayer, charity, or intellectual perception), is it possible that we can attain here on earth a religious level so pure that we have really "surpassed" the stage of sacramental practice? In other words, is sacramental practice a beginning to which there should succeed another phase in which we would live our Christian life "in depth" and in which "Christ would radiate in all our acts," etc.? Are there two things to be distinguished: sacramental practice and, on the other hand, what we might call an *authentic Christian life?*

Against this idea, it is the object of these pages to proclaim loudly that *there is nothing else for us to do but to receive the sacraments.*

What is the principle that will enable us to understand why it is impossible to do without the sacraments? Isn't it charity that counts above all?

We must mention immediately that the apparent opposition between charity and practicing one's religion is based on a number of illusions that are quite difficult to uproot. The greatest illusion concerns charity itself. We have a hard time admitting that *charity is absolutely, radically, and desperately foreign to us.* We hardly pay attention to some of Christ's words like: "If *you who are evil,* know how to give to your children . . ." (Mt. 7:11). These words show us how wrong we are to be overly sure of ourselves. To be good,

purely and simply (and we are not talking here about supernatural mysticism), is quite another thing from giving good
things to our children and to those whom we love: it is *a
divine privilege.* When we examine the lives of saints to discover true goodness, to know just to what point we have "to
turn the other cheek," "not judge," "hold one's tongue,"
etc., perhaps we will begin to suspect that charity must be
infused in us like a new life by divine omnipotence, of which
the miracles of the Gospel are a figure. It is the same for us:
we must be reborn to charity, as a paralyzed or a dead person is resurrected to life. "Oh God, create a new heart in
me!" (Ps. 51:12).

So long as we have not grasped to what point we are paralyzed or dead men, we are unable to attain the threshold
of the mystery of the sacraments, in the same way as we have
not attained the threshold of salvation so long as we have
not felt a need as great as our need for air. The ensemble of
processes by which God resurrects us is called the Seven Sacraments. The correct use we make of them is the "practice"
of the Christian life; the incorrect use is mere routine. Not
to use the sacraments is one of the most pernicious forms of
pharisaism. In ancient times, pharisaism consisted in glorify-
ing oneself by means of practices; but the temptation of
modern pharisaism is to do away with practices by trying to
go beyond them.

Therefore, when we try to go beyond religious practice,
we are trying to reach a state in which we no longer have
need for these material processes, this visible regulation, to
nourish ourselves with the life of God.

This state exists. It is the "beatific life," the definitive
possession of God, giving us the fullness of life and the assurance that we can never again lose it, tearing us away from

the prosaic and apparently routine conditionings of this life below. For this reason, when we think that we have out-grown the sacraments, we are engaging in a new form of man's tendency to pretend that he can lift himself above his condition. To love without "effort" is a heavenly privilege, which we are always tempted to reach for by ourselves. Be-hind disdain for the sacraments there lies hidden this old disdain for the body and, consequently, for man, which ani-mated the Manicheans and which even today is the inspira-tion for Platonists and Angelists of every kind.

When we refuse the path which faith proposes as the way to love, we sin not only against the truth and humility of the human condition, but against God, repeating again the first sin. This is why every abandonment which thinks itself noble because it is dictated by a thirst for God—for God sought beyond the priests and routine—and which wants to find him in sincerity of heart, is not so excusable as we might sometimes affirm when we attribute it to a thirst for authen-tic spirituality.

It is not a matter of knowing more or less whether we are "spiritual," more or less authentic, but whether *we believe in God's Word:* "Anyone who does eat my flesh and drink my blood has eternal life, . . . for my flesh is real food and my blood is real drink" (Jn. 6:54–55). If God has really said this, there are no sublime aspirations that can ever dispense with it. And observing it is simply "to practice" like the least of the faithful.

REMARKS CONCERNING METHOD

Theological reflection on the sacraments is among the richest reflections of Christian faith. We do not want to be satisfied here with merely extracting the sugar and flavor, but we must also broach the *actual* problems of sacramental practice under three aspects, being careful to show how these aspects are joined.

We purposely have not isolated them by presenting a chapter of Biblical theology, one of speculative theology, and another of pastoral theology. Such dissociation is illusory where the sacraments are concerned, because they are made for life: all reflection on the sacraments is simultaneously Biblical, theological, and pastoral, or it is nothing.

These are the viewpoints which have guided our reflection:

1. The difficulties and questions of modern man

The mystery of the sacraments has not been proposed to us in order to elaborate theories, but to help us to really encounter God.

What is the real necessity of the sacraments?

How are they rooted in our daily life?

What are the relationships between the world of our culture (with everything it contains of the imaginative, intellectual, or affective order, including our habits of work, our leisure, instinctive forces and moral conventions) and the universe of the sacraments?

To what exactly does the Paschal mystery correspond?

2. The fundamental notions contained in Scripture

What intuitions, particularly in St. Paul and St. John, give us the essentials concerning the mystery of the sacraments?

How can we understand what they mean when they speak of incorporation into Christ?

3. *The traditional practice of the Church in its liturgy and theology*

What should we think of the sacraments' effectiveness? Of their "independent" operation? What should we think of the sacramental character of the baptized? What are the principal faults in our sacramental practice, etc.?

Thus, we will begin by listening to the implicit questions which the Spirit of God poses to us by means of the difficulties and the hopes of modern man regarding the sacraments. Shouldn't the uneasiness which men feel be the first thing we listen to in order not to be mistaken about God?

1 The Value of Distress

Without spending too long on the difficulties which modern man experiences in face of the sacraments, it is useful to recall that these difficulties are very real despite the Council's efforts for renewal. There are many ways to summarize the obstacles to sacramental practice. Everyone is talking about them today. We will be satisfied to enumerate a few quite simply.

When man and God encounter each other, it is quite natural that there should be distances to be surmounted: it is from this disproportion that man's difficulties with regard to the sacraments are born.

We can note first of all a distance between faith which supposes a personal going forth, an interior commitment, and the sacraments which have perhaps been accepted in a largely traditional way: we were baptized because it was the family custom, we made our First Communion because it was the custom in our milieu, our community, etc. Does this mean that faith will progress in proportion to the rhythm of this practice? The question poses itself as soon as we leave our traditional milieu. Then appears the distance between the sacraments merely linked to one generation or to the habits of a family or a parish milieu, and personal faith.

There is also another gap between the way in which the sacraments are presented to us, and what today nourishes our

understanding and our sensitivity. It is quite evident that
the language and the images of our technical universe, of
information, and of publicity, are nearer to us and speak to
us more immediately than do the sometimes curtailed gestures and the foreign language of the liturgy. It is a great
help to be able to speak English rather than Latin, but nevertheless the language of the sacraments can appear quite dated
to someone who is seeking God.

We must finally acknowledge another no less real distance,
between the ministers of these sacraments and those who receive them. Often, even minimum contact and human sym-
pathy is cruelly missing, due to lack of time, fatigue, or a
perhaps inevitable incomprehension on the part of the priest,
when it is the merciful and peaceful presence of Christ we
look for in the sacraments.

To these almost inevitable and very real distances, we
must add the difficulties which proceed from the spectacle
presented by the failure of many who do regularly receive
the sacraments to live accordingly.

The members of the Church are very happy to have rediscovered in the modern world certain great values which seem
to be their allies for the renewal of religious practice. This
is profoundly true. The two principal values are, first of all,
the rediscovery of common life, the community, the assembly, the Church as a communion; and, secondly, the rediscovery of the role of the imaginative, of symbols, of the fact
that the life of our spirit is rooted in flesh.

We have quite evidently sloughed off Cartesianism. We
know better now that our life is not governed only by clear
and distinct ideas and that the real is not always clearly apprehended. We must give place to the power which symbols
have and on which the sacraments rest.

Our civilizations are also evidently teaching us not to isolate ourselves. Each one of us finds himself the tributary of a totality, of a community, which is true only to the degree it opens itself to all the communities seeking unity. Non-Christians are themselves seeking a "mystical body." And we have understood that the Church is our milieu of life and that we do not have to invent our faith, but that we receive it from this living community which gives us the means for access to God.

The symbol and the assembly, given their due again, permit us to live the sacraments better.

But we have to go still farther and ask ourselves whether there are other values in the modern world, stronger and more characteristic of it, which are the real signposts to the sacraments, and thus God's real accomplices.

There certainly exists an ineffable harmony between the sacraments and human nature, a merciful harmony, but it is very possible that it may remain invisible to us because it is founded on a concept of man quite foreign to our humanism and desire for human fulfillment. An unheard of conversion would be necessary for us to accept an idea of human nature which is as poor and also as real as the one to which the sacraments are adapted.

And nevertheless, our age has become sharply aware of certain values indispensable to real understanding of this harmony. Our times are privileged in more than one way to rediscover the life of the sacraments. We find ample proof for this in the vitality of the liturgical movement.

We know better now not only that civilizations perish, but also that man's condition is *a wounded condition,* a condition of distress.

We feel more than ever *the need for dialogue.* In a thousand circumstances of modern life—tourism, the development of communications and the diffusion of thought, etc.—we are rediscovering that "dialogue" is central.

Finally, we know better now that our life cannot be considered in the abstract, taking little account of the future, of personal development, or of the power of self-determination for which we are responsible. We know that *each one of us ends up in a history* inextricably linked to that of our brothers. Time is not exterior to our life.

Distress, dialogue, history. We must ask ourselves what relationship exists between these conditions of our life and the sacraments.

Long before existentialism and the research of sociologists accustomed us to the idea that man's situation is one of despair, we were quite aware that the human condition is an unstable one. The major economic upheavals and their philosophers, the revolutions and their prophets, had already attracted our attention to the notion of the human condition as a *wounded* condition. In this proposition there is recognition of a value and this is the value of distress. Thanks to it, something of true evangelical piety, such as the great saints felt toward the human race, has passed into the vision of men; and a bit of Christian pity has passed into philosophy, taking philosophy as the way a man has of seeing himself and seeing things. This should normally prepare us to understand better the greatness and the truth of the remedy which God's pity offers us.

Actually, those who are the most sensitive to man's agony are also, very often, those who seem deaf to the divine response of the sacraments. (For example, we might ask what place the sacraments have in the universe of some Christian existentialists.)

Perhaps the most precious opening which our century has to offer to God's intervention is this: humanity today is descending into such extreme anguish that the bare presentation of a truth, however evident, is no longer sufficient. We cannot accept being saved by an abstract truth, even if it is a very beautiful truth, unless it is the fruit of a religious *experience* to its very depths[1] and unless it is presented as a *personal witness* of salvation.[2]

In a recent interview about his conversion Henri-Georges Clouzot, the director of *La Vérité, Mystère Picasso,* and *Diaboliques,* told his story:

Everything began with a feeling of spiritual discomfort. The trial of Vera's [his wife's] death was terrible, but I never thought to look for consolation in the idea of the soul's immortality, in the idea that we would meet again in another world. No! At that time I was very far from hope in the beyond, but I felt that Camus and Sartre, after having given me much to think about, brought me no more and that finally the philosophy of the absurd ended in a dead-end.

So I told myself that since there is no supernatural salvation, I must find a salvation within this life, in other words, a way of being at one with myself without asking for any other recompense. So I began to read. I read Huxley, Plato. . . . Then, quite accidentally, I came across the work of Simone Weil. Through the example of her life, the density of her writings, through her theological explanation of evil and the suffering of the innocent, through her profound faith, simultaneously active and contemplative, and her way of loving her neighbor more than herself, by Christ and not for Christ, through all of this, I thought that perhaps there was a way. Her commentary on the *Pater* which she recited when she was exhausted with fatigue in the vineyards of the free zone at the beginning of the occupation, the diary in the factory, everything pierced me. I felt that I was being personally addressed. Unreasonably, no doubt, but I am a proud man. But then, isn't everyone addressed in his time and in his special circumstances?

I discovered that Faith is not something that we can discuss abstractly, but rather something that we live or do not live. I began with an intellectual questioning, until the day I noticed that prayer brought me much more. Much more, directly. But I began with an extremely vague prayer which was not even the prayer of Abraham, because when Abraham said, "Here I am!" to God, he believed totally in a unique God. I did not. I faced an unknown God. I said, "If you exist, give me light."

Another thing that helped me was the lack of proof for God's existence. A hidden God. For me, this lack of proof was the first proof: because if God respects man, he should want a free response; he would not put us under the obligation of believing in him.

I think that I committed the real sin when I was fifteen or sixteen years old, the sin against the Spirit which is a reflection of original sin. It is the desire to be oneself by oneself.

And the interviewer asked him, "All alone?" And Clouzot answered, "Yes, all alone."

"I will bring distress on them to see if they will find me then" (Jer. *10:18*).

Isn't it normal to fear moments of deep insight and distress? And isn't the refusal to recognize our wounded condition *the* great sign of prolonged adolescence and immaturity? Consider, in contrast, the attitudes of "men of faith," men "according to God's heart": Abraham, David, Jeremiah, who knew distress and knew enough to recognize their inability to save themselves. Still, aren't they brought to this attitude despite their will and their instinct which, by itself, tended

to leave them in illusion? (Cf., for example, in the life of
Moses: Ex. 2:11–15; 3:11–12; 4:10; 5:22–23.)

Doesn't the recognition of our condition already imply a
call from God? Don't the sacraments therefore appear like an
answer to the question which God asks us in secret?

This call almost always takes on disturbing forms: for
Agar, it is the jealousy of men and flight into the desert
(Gen. 21:8–21); the same was true for Elias (I Kings 19:1–8);
for the people of Israel it was exile (Baruch 2:30 to 3:8); for
David, it consisted in terrible events within his very family:
temptation and adultery, then the death of the new-born
child, which brought David to ask the question that would
dominate his entire life, "Will God take vengeance?" Then
there are all the familiar events: one of his sons violates his
sister and is killed by his brother, Absalom; and then Absalom, whom David loved, revolts against his father and begins
a war against him, to be finally killed in the last battle,
despite David's desire to save him (II Sam. 12:19). And we
must understand in the same spirit Osee's despair in his conjugal experience (Osee 2).

Don't we almost always discover God's call by discovering
our distress? In the story of the prodigal son, for example,
the father becomes a father to his son only after the latter
has experienced his inability to obtain happiness by himself
and to organize his own life all alone (Lk. 15:11–32).

What attitude should we have in face of this experience?
Compare in the Bible the attitudes of Saul and David (for
Saul, read I Sam. 13:8–14; 14:36–46; 18:8–12; 18:20–30;
28:7–15; for David, II Sam. 6:17–19; 12:13–23; 15:24–26;
18:1 to 19:2). Both of them succumb to their weakness and
discover their wounds, but for Saul, it is nothing but a new
occasion for pride and self-sufficiency: after breaking with

God he tries to reconcile himself, to buy him at any cost, even by magic; for David, it is an occasion to truly discover God: he does not try "to assure himself on his grace" by himself, to save himself by his own powers, but he discovers that he becomes attached to God by accepting that he needs him.

Why so many unexpected burdens and temptations in our existence? Why so many difficulties and darknesses? Why, for example, this burden of sexuality or of injustice, if not to oblige us from within to be unable to order our existence all alone? Why so many failures, if not, finally, so that we cannot do without a Savior.

When God brings man to agony, isn't it always for an increase of love? "In the country of their exile they will take all this to heart and acknowledge that I am the Lord their God. I will give them a heart and an attentive ear . . ." (Baruch 2:29–35). Isn't this the meaning of every exile? What forms do exile and agony take in our life? Do we know how to discover under their negative appearance the invitation extended to us to recognize the divine presence?

The first signpost which our civilization sets up pointing toward the sacraments, almost without knowing it, is this recognition of human nature's wounded condition. And this perspicacity is shown as well by the prophets of God's absence, like Nietzsche and Kafka, as by believers like Kierkegaard[3] or Simone Weil. It is not a question of baptizing or requisitioning every blasphemer to announce the Christian message, but we must have the loyalty to recognize that it was useful that some of them should demythologize the insufficient solutions and facile pacifications by vividly discovering the wound of our existence and, therefore, our need for a savior; and this is a contribution of very great value.

The world-vision proposed, for example, by a film-producer like Fellini in some of his films, is not very far from the world-vision of Pascal. They have incredible insights into man's confusion! We cannot easily forget such visions of the world.[4]

Once again, we do not intend to stop at the witness of non-Christians: serious reading of those who have expressed this confusion with the greatest genius, as Jaspers (in his book, *The Spiritual Situation of Our Times*) or Heidegger (in *Roads Leading Nowhere*), dispose us to hear some of the most insistent cries of the Bible: "I will bring distress on them to see if they will find me then!" Can't we read this same thing in what Malraux has written: "The most urgent task of the twentieth century is to reinvent its gods"?

And yet, it seems that we are still on the road. We often feel great sadness when we see that this harmony—if we can call it harmony—between the wounded condition of human nature and the life of the sacraments, the mystery of salvation they propose to us, is in fact too little perceived by our contemporaries[5] and that this fever which agitates them still remains very far from the point of maturation where they would finally be glad to return to the living water. Why is this?

There are undoubtedly two reasons: one is to be attributed not to the active, but to the passive aspect of today's mentality, and the second can be attributed to the modesty of the sacraments.

In the beginning, we are tempted to get rid of the doubt, the uneasiness, the agony, by interpreting as simply a crisis of growth this distress which we sometimes feel about ourselves and the future: we feel caught between a pitiless tendency to pessimism and the desire not to take too good a look at its true cause in order to find a reason to be optimistic. We interpret all the present confusion as a biologico-social phenomenon on the margin of an irresistible, explosive, and triumphant evolution. It is normal to hesitate. Our times are characterized by an intensification of both tendencies: optimism and pessimism; but a Christian cannot consciously evolve *with serenity* from one excess to the other.

Which tendency is at fault? It is not optimism, it is not hope. Nevertheless, we cannot in the name of this optimism list agony as growth when it is really due to man's weakness, to his wounded condition, to the ruptures and limitations which sin has produced in us. It is a very facile game, and a serious one for Christians, to evolve with a kind of unconsciousness from agony to optimism, baptizing everything belonging to the modern spirit, without taking account of the fact that there is incompatibility. This oversight dispenses with and at the same time *prevents the agony from reaching its logical conclusion which would be to demand a Savior.* We do not have the right to answer a concrete agony by an abstract optimism, even if it is that of the Omega point. With all due justice to Père Teilhard de Chardin, few authors have expressed as rigorously as Père Régamey[6] this illusion which makes us flee from the question that God poses to us in our distress and thereby *lose* the real source of our hope. "He takes no pleasure in abasing and afflicting the human race" (Lam. 3:33).

Finally, there is another reason why it is difficult for us to perceive a harmony between the sacraments and the human condition: it is because the signs and the sacramental rites themselves are too simple and poor. They are designed precisely to be within our reach and to help us in our daily life: we have to admit that it is possible for us to escape distress gradually by substituting, with the help of Christ, a kind of thirst in the place of despair and a kind of searching in the place of agony. This excludes anything artificial.

But it requires a singular humility to put less confidence in the effectiveness of our human efforts and the construction of a new world than in the acceptance of hope. We would much rather accomplish this passage from death to life all alone. It costs us to frankly and flatly admit that salvation comes to us from Another through the reception of the sacraments. That such a great paschal mystery should be enclosed in such modern realities disturbs us. Our faith finds it hard to surmount the difficulty of identifying the sacraments with the living Jesus Christ, the only Savior. We will spend more time on this later in the book. There is no other answer to our distress than Jesus Christ crucified and resurrected, and no other theological justification for the sacraments.

Only God saves. And if God saves, then everything is easy. But we have a very hard time admitting it, because we are not humble enough.

NOTES

1. Cf. M.-D. Chenu, *La foi dans l'intelligence* (Paris; 1964), "Anthropologie et liturgie," pp. 309–321.

2. Cf. O.-A. Rabut, *La vérité de l'action* (Paris: Ed. du Cerf, 1961) and G. Morel, *Le sens de l'existence selon saint Jean de la Croix*, vols. II and III (Paris: Ed. Aubier, 1960).

3. Cf. Kierkegaard, *La difficulté d'être chrétien*, Introduction and choice of texts by J. Colette, O.P., coll. "Chrétiens de tous les temps"

(Paris, 1964). Cf. especially the second part of the introduction, pp. 34–88, and the third part of the texts: "De l'angoisse à l'amour," pp. 175 ff.

4. Cf. Fellini's statements in G. Agel and D. Delouche, *Les chemins de Fellini,* coll. "7e art" (Paris, 1956), pp. 104–105, 128–129, 158–159.

5. We quote Sartre's significant comment when he criticized those who would give a religious terminus to human uneasiness, like Kierkegaard and Jaspers (and he knocked at the right door): "We could already ask whether Kierkegaard drew his readers into the depths of subjectivity for the sole reason of making them discover the unfortunate situation of man without God. . . . Jaspers plays with his cards on the table: he did nothing other than comment on his master, and his originality consists principally in putting certain themes into relief and hiding others. For example, the transcendent seems at first absent from this thought, but it is there; we learn to feel it through our failures, it is their profound meaning. Jaspers, who says nothing about Revelation, brings us to that pure and formal subjectivity which discovers itself and discovers transcendence through its defeats. . . . Meditating on failure is perfectly suited to a partially dechristianized bourgeoisie that regrets faith because it has lost confidence in its rationalist and positivist ideology. Even Kierkegaard thought that every victory is suspect because it turns man away from himself. Kafka took up this theme again in his *Journal,* and we can find some truth in it because in a world of alienation the individual victor does not recognize himself in his victory and because he becomes a slave in it. But what matters to Jaspers is to draw from it a subjective pessimism and to make it flow out into a theological optimism which does not dare to pronounce its own name; in effect, the transcendent remains veiled and proves itself only by its absence; we will not surpass the pessimism, we will have our *presentiment* of the reconciliation while remaining on the level of an insurmountable contradiction and a total rending" (J.-P. Sartre, *Critique de la raison dialectique,* vol. I, Ed. Gallimard, 1960, pp. 21–22).

We must therefore conclude (as Sartre has remarked elsewhere) to "the terrible catastrophe which has befallen some representatives of the animal kingdom: thought."

6. Cf. *Portrait spirituel du chrétien* (Ed. du Cerf), pp. 441–442. Also,

Chap. 22: "A quoi bon? L'appréhension actuelle du malheur"; Chap. 8: "Voir ce que l'on voit"; Chap. 12: "Nécessité du pessimisme optimiste." And cf. Père Régamey's index, under *optimisme* and *pessimisme*.

2 The Revolution of Dialogue

> He who withdraws from the commerce of men
> is either a brute or a god.
>
> ARISTOTLE

We find ourselves continually using the phrases community life, necessity of dialogue, attention to others, etc. But we have to admit that we do not possess the virtues they express to a very great degree. To be sure, it is quite true that one of the great accomplishments of the civilization and world in which we live is that it has rediscovered the meaning of human relations, rediscovered that there is no truth for man if he places himself outside of dialogue.

Our contemporaries have underlined not only the agony of the human condition, but also the dignity of the person. We should not too quickly condemn man's interest in himself, his anthropocentrism, his discovery that he is a "subject," that he is the center and measure of everything. Rather than distrust ourselves, we do better to ask if these demands men make are really for Christians questions posed by the Spirit of God, and therefore bearers of light. When we interest ourselves in man as a subject, self-subsistent and set over against "the other" and "others," we are making a step which leads us inevitably to interest in dialogue. Some might think that when we interest ourselves in man we are removing ourselves from the "transcendent and objective" God. Since the

time of the Renaissance, we have often enough accused thinkers of every type of doing so.

But *God is dialogue* and he wants to attract us to himself
in a dialogue which is the image of his own. So we cannot be
indifferent about whether or not, or to what degree, we exist
in our human condition by means of a dialogue.

We are quite aware that today, when a man refuses to
listen to others, whether it be to a call for help from his
parish, or from a distressed section of his city, or from those
with whom he lives, from his children or his union, if he
refuses himself to others, it is because he refuses himself to
himself. That is an ageless truth. But we must go further
when we speak of the current interest in "dialogue."

We are witnesses to a real revolution in human history
and in our way of life, and this revolution is irreversible. It
comes from the weight and importance taken on by *communication,* which is changing our old frames of reference and
creating a new way of being. The possibilities of mass media
and communication between persons are increasing to gigantic
proportions; moving over short or long distances is gradually becoming a possibility for everyone. Everyone is regis-
tered in a vast network of relations. Established values and
laws, like family roots, have lost their importance; a greater
liberty linked to a still greater uncertainty governs the conduct of each person. Every man finds himself more and more
influenced by a dense, varied, changing network of persons
and groups.

Man lives today in a state of dialogue. If we might compare the men of ancient civilization to the gyroscope which
finds its equilibrium by turning on its familial and personal
axis, we can consider modern man as an open radar oriented
by his relation to others.[1] In this way, we learn that there is

no man "in himself," but only men who feel the need for or are in a state of dialogue.

Are we at least capable of being honest with the exigencies and laws of dialogue? As Christians, we are very much in the habit of disguising everything in the name of the sublime! Take an example: we often denature the reality of death, either in name of the paschal mystery ("Death is behind us," "Death, where is your victory?," "Death has been vanquished by Christ," etc.), or by recourse to a certain way of looking at death as the symbol or effect of sin, or by invoking values we call "spiritual." In this way, we come to no longer assign to it—and therefore no longer to time and its limits—its actual, real weight in our life. We come to convince ourselves under the pretext of spirituality that the fact of being mortal no longer defines our daily manner of existing or our relationship with life at every instant: death becomes no more than a future event which is not very important to the Christian, something of the past, behind us, because Christ has overcome it.

We are using death as an example because it is one of the most habitual cases of this disguising of realities. We must perhaps say the same thing about the truth of dialogue. We approve of it, certainly; but, because we are in the habit of holding the truth, of always "knowing something already" (as Merleau-Ponty said of Catholics), can we say that we accept the astonishing purifications and exactions which human dialogue presupposes? If we answer this question honestly, we can immediately see the place which the sacraments are meant to hold in our life, because by their very nature they are a dialogue.

We know what courage real dialogue takes. We can recognize what confidence it takes in the greatest men, as, for example, when St. Thomas thanks his opponents: "I will be quite happy if someone wants to write against my solutions. There is no better way to discover the truth and to refute error than in defending one's self against opponents" (St. Thomas Aquinas, *On the Perfection of the Christian Life*); or again: "Just as in the courts no one can judge who has not heard the arguments of both parties, so also it is necessary for the philosopher to hear all the thinkers and their conflicting evidence, to have more resources in forming his judgment" (*Commentary on the Metaphysics*). "A great philosophy is not one against which there is nothing to say. It is one which has said something. . . . [It] is not one which hands down judgments; it is perhaps one which renders services. It is in any case one which *introduces instances. . . .*" (Péguy).

An honest and sincere dialogue brings us to recognize the share of truth which another person holds, whether or not he be our adversary. "I do not seek to convict my adversary of error, but to unite myself with him in a higher truth" (Lacordaire). "All religion possesses a ray of light which we should neither scorn nor extinguish. . . . All authentic religious truth is a dawning of faith, and we wait for it to open into daybreak and into the radiant splendor of Christian wisdom" (Paul VI, Easter message, 1964).

But we who are neither geniuses nor saints must recognize that we have quite a long way to go before reaching the conditions of true dialogue. Biologists tell us that pigeons are happy and in good endocrinal equilibrium only if they are two's. So someone tried the experiment of putting a lone pigeon in a cage containing a mirror, and the bird was perfectly happy: he had the illusion that there was another pigeon with him; all he needed was the image of the other.

Aren't we very often like this pigeon in our dialogues, happy to have someone in front of us, merely because he can reflect our image?

Let us not be too hasty to condemn ourselves, as long as we see the point. It is quite normal to want to surpass one's limitations and to need to extend one's self so long as we remain on our own ground; and to want to profit from our double who is a little different from ourself but like enough for us to rest comfortably in ourself.

Marcel Proust wrote an impressive page on this subject. We see the young Proust in the gardens where he plays with Gilberte whom he met on the Champs Elysées, and with whom he is falling in love.

And when the time came for the postman I said to myself, that evening as on every other: "I'm going to have a letter from Gilberte, she is going to tell me, at last, that she has never ceased to love me. . . ."

Every evening I would beguile myself into imagining this letter, believing that I was actually reading it, reciting each of its sentences in turn. Suddenly I would stop, in alarm. I had realized that, if I was to receive a letter from Gilberte, it could not, in any case, be this letter, since it was I myself who had just composed it. . . . Even if, by an almost impossible coincidence, it had been precisely the letter of my invention that Gilberte had addressed to me of her own accord, recognizing my own work in it, I should not have had the impression that I was receiving something that had not originated in myself, something real, something new, a happiness external of my mind, independent of my will, a gift indeed from love.[2]

And us? What is the value of our dialogues? To be sure, we accept conversation with the "other," but on condition that he conform to the image we want to receive, so long as he not be truly "other," but remains this reassuring reflection, without personality, without newness, without anything unforeseen.[3] In that case, what are we really listening to?

On the other hand, men who are capable of dialogue witness to such great spiritual force! Everyone of us has met some such person. We can think of Dostoyevsky whose genius created characters who are among the most significant. Believers or unbelievers, they cannot defend themselves from questions which confront them. Even the most deeply mysterious, like Ivan Karamazov, know that they are themselves only when they are searching for light. They cannot live without explaining themselves; all of them, not only Alyosha, need a guide, a starets, someone to answer in their dialogue. Dostoyevsky makes them call on the light of another, though it be an opponent, in the expectation that this other will reveal them to themselves. Each discovers little by little that he can do nothing else but listen and beg others to listen to him. Each one seems drawn, whether he wants it or not, to go to the very end of questions he asks despite all his distress, and he discovers that there is no other way to escape than by listening to the questions of other people.

And these are the greatest scenes of world literature: a drunken father, Marmaladov, obliges his daughter Sonia to prostitute herself; an assassin falls asleep beside a prince who is in love with his mistress; a young monk, Alyosha, brings his brother's companion to the brink of tears because for the first time in his life someone listens to him. . . . What a universe! And it is one of the closest to the Gospel that has ever been created. These characters do not present us with a rational world, or an Aristotelian one, or a virtuous one;

and nevertheless this universe is Christian because in Dostoyevsky there is nothing but dialogue; and this dialogue, because it goes right to the very depths of pity and comprehension, ascends all the way to God and his mercy and thus finds, virtually perhaps, the equilibrium of Christian wisdom.[4]

We know today that the man who refuses to listen to others refuses himself to himself (cf. St. Thomas, II-II, q. 188, a. 8). Sartre's famous formula, "L'enfer c'est les autres" (Hell is other people), is ambiguous enough that its author thought it a good idea to explain it.[5]

THE SACRAMENTS ACCOMPLISH DIALOGUE

The attention we pay to man makes us sensitive to this aspect of the Christian mystery that on one hand, God is a living person, and on the other hand, man is made to enter into dialogue with him like a living person. When we say that Christianity is not only a religion but a faith, we mean that this religion is not only defined by a certain abstract *Credo* to which the Christian is obliged to adhere, but that faith, being the assimilation of a message, is at the same time a living encounter. There is no act of faith except in an actual Pentecost, because the Christian can never isolate *that-which-is-said-to-him* from *Him-who-says-it-to-him*. No less than for faith, can there be sacraments except within a dialogue.[6]

The necessity to use the sacraments during our Christian life is rooted in God's desire to save us by dialogue and only by dialogue. The sacraments oblige us step by step to enter into this mystery of communion and to accept this dialogue. This is why the sacraments are so easy to approach, without suffering routine or resorting to magic. Thus, for example, if the sacrament of Penance includes the obligation to confess one's sins, it is in order to seek pardon from *someone* in a dialogue.

In the same way, when we receive communion at Mass, we discover that the Christian contemplative life is not a solitary life, but a life with Someone, which binds us in a mystery of communion, simultaneously descending by the Word and ascending by the sacrifice. The necessity of receiving Communion is the necessity of being two in our contemplation; one, Christ, absorbs the life of the other in giving him his flesh. The dialogue of the sacraments does not come primarily from us, from our need to escape solitude, to call for help; but it comes from God's will to accomplish work for two.

According to the greatest of the philosophers, like Plato and Plotinus, we are called at best to become spectators in a divine city, spectators of a Good of which we can attain an idea by contemplating what escapes this present order: the heavens and their numbers and sometimes the city or the virtue of men. According to St. Paul, we are much more than spectators, "We are fellow workers with God" (I Cor. 3:9). And this is for him the decisive newness of Christianity: love did not permit God to remain alone. God invites each one of us to take part in his work, in communicating salvation, in such a real way that he presents himself to us *as if he wanted to be overcome by our intervention.* And this is not in order to "pretend." God presents himself to all of his witnesses in such a way that it is really they—it is we—who in a way answer God's prayer.

This lesson is apparent everywhere in the Gospel at each one of our Lord's encounters, as well as in the Old Testament. What does Christ do when the Canaanite woman comes to him? He obliges her to fight to obtain her daughter's cure and to almost force his hand (Mt. 15:21–28). What does the angel make Jacob do at the ford of Jabbok? He presents himself all night long as one who wants to be overcome by his friend, to such a degree that Jacob is persuaded that God leaves a real part to his cooperation (Gen. 32:23–31). In the same way, Abraham before the destruction of Sodom (Gen. 18:16–33) and Moses after the adoration of the golden calf (Ex. 32:11–14) discover that God is infinitely nearer than they had believed. In these dialogues, God presents himself as one who does not want to do without us what he has decided to do with us: "shall I conceal from Abraham what I am going to do?" (Gen. 18:17).

God wants us to force his hand; he does not change, but he has intended beforehand and expects that we take part in his work as free men who are sources of their own destiny. He wants to accomplish this work in answer to his friends: this is the dignity of the sacraments and the assurance they give us.

GOD HIMSELF IS DIALOGUE

We must go even further: we are more than cooperators with a God who would otherwise be solitary. God himself is dialogue, and he wants to draw us to himself within this dialogue. For this reason, it is absolutely false to define the sacraments only from man's viewpoint. Man's dialogue with God must be defined as a trinitarian dialogue with echoes in the human heart. St. Paul unceasingly repeats the fact that there can be no relation to God outside of the Spirit: "No one can say, 'Jesus is Lord' unless he is under the influence of the Holy Spirit" (I Cor. 12:3). "The Spirit too comes to help us in our weakness. . . . The Spirit Himself expresses our plea in a way that could never be put into words" (Rom. 8:26). "The proof that you are sons is that God has sent the Spirit of his Son into our hearts: the Spirit that cries, 'Abba, Father'" (Gal. 4:6; cf. Rom. 8:15).

So long as we have not grasped this insight, the essence of the Mass and the sacraments escapes us. What is the meaning of the Canon of the Mass? The *Preface?* "Praise to you because you have sent us your Son who has come . . ." The *Consecration?* ". . . Who on that holy night took bread and wine so that with him we might return to you . . ." The *Our Father* and the *Communion?* ". . . So that with him, we dare to say 'You are Our Father' and to come to your table."

We are familiar with St. Augustine's boldness when, to explain these affirmations of Scripture and the practice of the Church, like the Our Father in the Mass, he went so far as to write: "In order that God might be praised well by man, God praised himself. . . . In order to be praised by his servants, isn't it he himself who sings his own praises?"

Therefore, it is important that we discover in our human condition to what point we exist by dialogue and communication, the very law of the spirit, as we indicated at the beginning of this chapter. The sacraments oblige us little by little to live not only with God *before* us, but to live in common with a *God-with-us.* We sometimes think that we have said everything there is to be said about God when we have affirmed that he pardons; but he has done much more for us—and each time that we receive the sacrament of Penance he does much more for us—because God has come to weep with the sinner, condemned among the condemned.

We will go a bit farther and suggest that the only real dialogue can be found in faith and the sacraments, and this for two reasons:

All of our experiences with human dialogue are limited, more or less self-interested, spoiled or artificial, as it were, vitiated, because we can never pretend to put ourselves in the place of the other. We cannot go outside of our poor skin and become external to ourself! This is why all our experiences of dialogue, even the most intimate and the most noble, are in a way radically false. It is a privilege reserved for heaven to be able to love the other "as he loves himself" with his own heart. Here below, we yearn for this encounter with the other and yearn for him who can teach it to us. And this is Jesus in whom the Father has all his pleasure. It is not a way of speaking, but the profound root of his existence, his reason for existing: "Word and Son." We must learn to read the terrible and efficacious realism of his presence—for us.

Jesus needs only to be who he is, that is, the Son of God, who revealed to us who the Father is and what it means to be his son. He himself is the exact, unique, and perfect filial relationship with God his Father. He is this filial relationship become body and soul, heart and face, prayer and sacrifice. He is this filial relationship suddenly become, for our opened eyes, revelation and liberation: revelation of what it is to be a son and to have a father, and liberation from all the caricatures of the father which had hopelessly imprisoned our filial consciousness.

Some of depth psychology's discoveries allow us to evaluate and formulate with amazing neatness what humanity was before the coming of the Son of God and what it still is before being healed by him. It is by means of the parental relationship lived by each child that this child-become-adult normally conceives his relation to God: and this results in the structure of the spirit created in a terrestrial and carnal condition. Generation after generation, alterations in this relationship are transmitted, indeed aggravated, with a terrible fatality. The child's fear, his need for security, his resentment, revolt and many other instinctive currents, impose an irremediable distortion in every filial relationship lived by men, and therefore in every concept they can form of the divine paternity.[7]

As a result, *where will they find a pure experience on which a true language and a true religion can be founded?* As minimal as this distortion may be in some persons, it is still too great not to forever prevent humanity from perceiving God's real characteristics and from entering into the pure filial relationship which consummates all justice and all religion. A deep psychological opaqueness, often unconscious, congenitally troubles our vision. In order to burst through this powerlessness and to break this fatality which are the proofs of sin, *it was necessary that one day somewhere humanity experience an authentic and pure filial relationship* in the integral transparency of the truth. The heart of a son still intact, preserved, a new heart, was necessary. There had to exist one day a consciousness of filiation to God that was psychoanalytically pure.

This was the consciousness of Christ, and, by an incomprehensible design of the divine love, this Christ was the true Son of God; he revealed not only the perfection of a natural religion, but the secret of supernatural sonship. In Christ's human soul, for the first time, there lived the true, right, perfect relationship of a son with his Father. In Christ's human soul was revealed to us how we can say, "Abba, Father!," without contaminating it with the cry of unconscious conflicts which irremediably disfigure the face of the Father to our eyes. So, "as we learned from our Savior, and according to his command, we dare to say: Our Father. . . ."

We have to add another reason: the sacraments are our teachers for our dialogue with men. God is the only one who for us certainly is "Other," but who is not "an" other. "In me he is more me than I am." So much the better if the tradition of the Church obliges us to a sacramental practice different from facing the mirror of a book or a meditation. God teaches me from within; he is not merely outside me, a formulation like any other. He is present. Because he is present in the very texture of my life, he does not merely face me. He is present. He is there in mercy when I extend mercy; he is in patience; he is in the cry that rises out of the burning recognition of my sins; and he is with the priest who pardons me. He is in the assembly of my brothers with whom I receive Communion at Mass; he is this assembly. He is with the bride and the groom who, in their marriage, share a love that transcends them.

Each sacrament exercises God's mercy toward me under a different aspect: a mercy which is paternal, fraternal, healing, preparing, faithful, fortifying . . . to make me love the other, the others, as God loves them.

It is true that our dialogue with God is terrible in its simplicity. It does not suffice to have rediscovered the general virtues of dialogue to eliminate the temptation of substituting something else for it when it is a question of our relationship with God. This is one of the major points in the pedagogy of our life: the temptation to fabricate our encounter with God ourselves or to think up alibis.

Marxism is meant to make us think of this. It is founded on the *homo faber* ("man the maker"), the man who con-

structs his own conditions for existence. It believes that the
depth of the mystery of man is a construction. And what
does Christianity have to say about this? The depth of the
mystery of man is a mystery of friendship, a sharing, a contemplation in a dialogue with Someone who surpasses it. I
cannot always construct my own conditions for existence;
one day or another I must recognize my own powerlessness.
I must accept God as I must accept my friends.

"If you are in ecstasy and your friend needs help, leave
your ecstasy and go bring him help. The God you leave is
less certain than the God you will find" (John Ruysbroeck).
The meaning of dialogue brings us to rediscover that in loving our brothers and in welcoming them we welcome God;
but of this too, if we are not careful, we risk making an alibi.
God also wants to be present in our life, and he wants us to
be as occupied with him as with our brothers. And we must
have the courage to confront his person through the persons
of our brothers, but not only under the pretext that they are
one with God. This is why someone who really understands
these things truly accomplishes the same interior act when
he receives Communion and when he receives his brother;
and to accomplish this act is to confront the mystery of God
in all truth.

The precept of fraternal love and the necessity of religious
practice correspond to the same obsession of God: that our
love be incarnated, that is, that it translate itself into action
and not consist only in words. God tells us not to flee from
his look by tying ourselves up with practices, but also not to
flee him by becoming all tied up in good works. The sacraments and charity are opposed only in the mind of a man
who is looking for an alibi. But they are really only one, like
the act of love, like the truth of dialogue. He who pretends

to love God and flees from his brothers, remains alone in himself and substitutes his own meditations for the reality of God's look which comes through his brothers. The man who asks for pardon by means of a simple interior movement, without humiliating himself before his brothers, is fleeing dialogue with God in another way; his consciousness of being humble seeks to supply for the bending of his heart before a real look.

This is why those who have truly loved God have wanted actual encounter with Christ really man. They knew enough to recognize in the Eucharist the truth of a spiritual encounter which is also between Christ and us an encounter of man with man. Therefore, to refuse that this encounter be physical at the same time as spiritual by means of the sacraments is to refuse that it be complete. The instinct of faith has never tolerated this. The sacraments bring us to a constant, real dialogue with the living God.

NOTES

1. On this point, among other works, cf. especially that of D. Riesman, *The Lonely Crowd* (New Haven: Yale University Press, 1950; 1961, paper).

2. Marcel Proust, *Swann's Way* (*Remembrance of Things Past*), trans. by C. K. Scott Moncrieff (New York: Modern Library, 1928). Reprinted with the permission of Random House, Inc.

3. Cf. Rapports et actes du Congrès de Louvain 1966 de l'Assoc. cath. intern. médico-psychologique, *La relation pastorale individuelle* (Paris: Ed. du Cerf, 1966 and 1967).

4. Cf. Romano Guardini's analyses in *l'Univers religieux de Dostoïevsky* (Paris: Ed. du Seuil).

5. "*Hell is other persons* has always been misunderstood. People have thought that I meant by this that our relationships with other people are always poisoned and that they are therefore forbidden relationships. But I mean quite a different thing. I mean that if our relationships with others are twisted and vicious, then the others can only be hell. Why? Because the others are basically what there is most important in ourselves for our own understanding of ourselves. When we think about ourselves, when we try to know ourselves, we are actually using knowledge which others already have of us. We judge ourselves with the means that the others have and that they have given us. The judgment of the other person always enters into anything I may say about myself. This means that if my relationships are bad, I place myself in a total dependence on others and therefore, actually, I am in hell because I depend too much on the judgment of the others. But this dos not mean that we cannot have relationships with others. *It only indicates the capital importance which all of the others have for each one of us*" (Preface to a recording of *Huit clos*, Deutsche Grammophon Gesellschaft, Archiv. littéraire, 43902–3).

6. We can read with profit E. Schillebeeckx's book, *Christ, the Sacrament of the Encounter with God* (New York: Sheed & Ward, 1963), and, by the same author, "Les sacrements, organes de la rencontre de Dieu" in *Questions théologiques aujourd'hui*, vol. II (Paris: Desclée de Brouwer, 1965). We also want to call attention to the importance of H. Urs von Balthasar's short work, *L'amour seul est digne de foi* (Paris: Ed. Aubier, coll. "Foi vivante," 1966), not only because it recapitulates the thought of one of the greatest theologians of our time, but especially because it shows us how, within an anthropocentric theology (i.e. a theology whose departure-point is man), we can give transcendence its place by means of a rigorous analysis of what love and dialogue are; cf. especially pp. 51–59 on intersubjectivity and the possible degradations of dialogue, pp. 62 ff. on the going-beyond which is inherent in all dialogue, pp. 68 ff. on the way in which God invites man to dialogue, pp. 93–136 on the consummation of this dialogue, encounter and adoration, and the sacraments' contemplative aspect.

7. Cf. J.-M. Pohier's analysis in his criticism of P. Ricoeur: "Au nom du Père," in *Esprit*, March–April 1966 (I. Psychanalyse, foi et philosophie. II. L'illusion de la religion selon Freud: la nostalgie du Père.

III. La foi sans illusion selon Ricoeur, le renoncement au Père. IV. Celui de qui toute paternité tire son nom.) Also cf. A.-M. Besnard, "Prière et paternité divine," in *La Vie Spirituelle,* January 1960, pp. 5-33.

3 Eternity Refound

God invents us with us.

E. MOUNIER

When you have a past, Vovone, you will see what a funny thing
it is. There are whole corners caved in, nothing left. On the
other hand, there are weeds pushed up here and there, though
we can't recognize anything there either. And then there are
places we find so beautiful that we picture them again every
year, sometimes with one color, sometimes with another, and it
ends up not resembling at all what it was. Without counting
what we thought very simple and without mystery while it was
happening, and which we have discovered was not so clear only
years later, like the times you pass by something you never even
noticed, then suddenly you notice it. . . . Ideas like those, even
very baroque ones, pop up everyday in everyone's head; you will
know that when you have my experience.[1]

This page which we have cited recalls one of the unavoid-
able conditions of our existence and of the dialogue in which
it ends: time. We are relearning today this dimension of our
life, which is duration. We are no longer willing to speak in
the abstract about our life or about the history of men. And
this greater attention to the reality of time and becoming is
an immense acquisition of our present civilization and a new
reason for better understanding the role of the sacraments.

A real change has occurred in our way of looking at what
we are and in our idea of what a man is. This change can be

expressed in one word: we now know better that our life is a
journey and that our destiny is a mystery of progression. To
be sure, it would be quite naive to believe that we have just
discovered this idea which was born before Christianity itself. One way or another, we are now finding it present in
each of the geniuses who have tried to ascertain precisely the
laws of Christian existence: whether it be Gregory of Nyssa
who chose the Exodus as the schema-type of the Christian
life,[2] or St. Bernard's idea of a return to God by the roads of
education and liberty,[3] or the importance which St. Thomas
Aquinas gives to the Platonic idea of process and return, or
St. John of the Cross' concept of an "ascent of Carmel."[4]

The thing that is new is not that we try to describe the
Christian life as a journey, but that this idea has now taken
first place. Return to the Bible, as well as what is most lucid
in modern philosophies, obliges us to understand that human
life, in becoming Christian, *finds a meaning for its movement forward.* For a Christian, life is not merely an unfolding, but a history which proceeds towards an encounter and
which requires being lived like a history; in other words, it
demands imperiously that the Christian be conscious of his
times. Christian life is a "Passover," that is, a passage towards
Someone, or it is nothing at all. If not, then we must recognize that "all the history of the world is a history of clouds
that construct, destroy, dissipate, and reconstruct themselves
in different combinations, without any more meaning or
importance in the world than in heaven" (Montherlant).

MAN AS A PROJECT

The sacraments should have all the more weight and truth
in our eyes in that they answer in a real and concrete way
the "uneasiness" which is the burden of our century.

Uncertain of everything, if not of our point of departure, we are free to think of the future according to our powers. No age has ever experienced such contradictions. Is this a time of agony —or of wonderful birth? The only things that remain constant are the amplitude and the depth of change. . . . *We are perpetual candidates for emigration,* for whatever new world comes along, so long as it does not resemble our own.[5]

And this continual menace of change can make us afraid. We should be lucid as to what these uprootings of modern man, his infidelities and instabilities, can involve; but it would be false and absolutely ridiculous to have nothing but this reflex of fear in face of change. We should rather be glad that a man today cannot live without taking account of this new situation: he has learned that it belongs to his nature to change. We can no longer approach a problem, whatever it may be, without beginning by examining its situation in relation to time.[6]

With his roots and stability menaced, man instinctively looks toward the future. He discovers that it is natural to live in a state of pro-ject and that it is his nature not only to simply look at the present but also to expect the future.

On another plane, all of Teilhard de Chardin's readers understand that this confrontation with time and becoming was precisely one of the principal objects of his reflection. He wanted to reconcile man with time and the evolution of time by showing him that he does not need to be afraid and that this condition of our life is a good one.

One thing that we can no longer doubt when we have read Teilhard is that we are advancing and that life has a meaning: it draws us along like a river hurrying on its course. A great thing is happening with us, around us, and each one of us is responsible for his part in each retardation or progress. *He shows us how to "commune with becoming."* As trying and desperate as this communion may sometimes be, we must realize that any other attitude resembles desertion. This thinking planet has reached the moment of essential choices. Perhaps its privilege among all the others is to bear the seal of Christ, the cross on which sorrow mixes with hope and which, planted at the supreme crossroads, shows humanity the true path, that of love.[7]

There certainly was reason for this perspective to be all-conquering. The past is no longer absent, and the present is primarily in project. We model the present on all of our past, and we model it on everything we are lacking and on everything we desire. We mentioned above that to refuse to be in this way "in circuit," is to refuse the very equilibrium of our condition, which is a dynamic equilibrium, the equilibrium of being born to advance, whose very life is progress.

"The age of the finished world is beginning," said Valéry. Not only, like the migratory bird, do we hold ourselves in equilibrium only when we are tending toward the future, but henceforth we live with a calculated future. Christopher Columbus sailed away and accepted the adventure without knowing the map of his voyage. We also are sailing on a voyage, and at every moment of our adventure, we draw up beforehand a "Plan" and the map for the voyage. Should we bemoan this or rather see in it the supreme nobility of man? It belongs to each person to give meaning to his voyage.

But what do the sacraments bring to this adventure? The answer to this question is impossible to understand so long as we have not experienced the discomfort of this situation of man.

We never achieve complete possession of ourselves; in the

depths of our nature, there is a wound which never quite heals, and it is forever impossible for us to recapitulate all of our duration. We are condemned to be continually on the march, and this is uncomfortable.

This discomfort can be summarized in two continual experiences we have in our life which are the cause of anguish: *uncertainty before the future* and *the irreversibility of the past*. And, as we shall see, this is exactly where the sacraments grasp our life.

Whatever our efforts in face of the future, we have a hard time escaping fear and it is therefore normal for us to try to evade it, either by illusion or by concluding to the absurdity of life and human history because they unfold in time which is headed toward death. As Christians, just as we are tempted to falsify dialogue because we are sure of holding the truth, we are also tempted to mask this fear of the future because we believe too easily that we have "eternal" life. But eternity is not only difficult, but impossible to imagine. It does us no good to say we are capable of it and that it will be our destiny; we cannot even figure out what it is. We are lacking a terminus, an end which resists and limits; and eternity—the key to our future—cruelly escapes our imagination. Our reason tells us that the idea of eternity is reasonable, but we fail everytime we attempt really to know what "it" will be.

We know only too well that not only civilizations are mortal. In every human life, time is a death as well as a birth. The acceptance of growing old as well as the instability of all the wagers we make on the future reaches what is most alive in us.

It is quite natural for us to try to escape, in one way or another, from this discomfort of time. At every moment of our life, we feel two temptations: to try to go outside of time and to "be resigned," or to give in to impatience and try to fulfill our desires ourselves. We all know impatience or scepticism; it is the paradox of Christian duration.

Impatience induces us to see nothing but the present task and the terrestrial organization of our life. We do not believe that we are really facing God unless we feel that we are "doing something." We want to "leap over Providence" and put off to later the expectation of this eternal life which surpasses us.

At the contrary pole, resignation tempts us. In name of the spiritual, we give up our daily tasks. In name of a pretended abandonment to Providence, the "spiritual" life serves as an excuse to run away from the necessary combat, as though the battle did not doubly concern us, since it begins eternity.[8]

In face of the future or the past, we all have to cure ourselves of the illness of fear. For us, the cure has a name: it is faith in the eternal life which has already begun. It is not simply an object of debate among theologians. Nothing will be true in our Christian life if we do not in deed and in truth believe in this eternal life and in the present existence of salvation. It is already here, the judgment is not for later. According to the thought of St. John and St. Paul, the Parousia is only the last act of what began at the time of our baptism.

"With God on our side who can be against us? . . . . Could anyone accuse those that God has chosen? *When God acquits,* could anyone condemn? For I am certain of this: neither death nor life, ... nothing that exists, nothing still to come, . . . nor any created thing, can ever come between us and the love of God" (Rom. 8:31 ff.). This is St. Paul's certitude and it is inseparable from the certitude of

our responsibility: "we are fellow workers with God" (I Cor.
3:9). At the same time, our assurance comes from the fact
that it is God who justifies and that everything comes from
God, and we also know that salvation will occur only for
those who commit themselves to this cooperation even to the
cross.

This is what is at stake in the sacraments. It is what we
call eschatology, the supreme accomplishment of time, which
commands the entire Christian life. By means of these sacraments, God proposes to surmount this obsession with time
and history. They do not suppress the discomfort of the present, but they permit the projects and dynamism of human
life to have a certitude: the certitude of victory and a purpose which cannot disappear. "God invents us with us"
(Mounier), God wants to espouse all of man's situations.
There is no experience of human life which escapes the plan
of the Incarnation if, by means of the sacraments, we are
willing to inscribe them in the only history which does not
pass away, that of the people of God, that of the Mystical
Body of Christ.

For a Christian, the only correct way of living his situation
in time—and it is a paradox—is as follows: the future has already begun, the past is not yet finished, salvation is being
accomplished by Jesus Christ. Everything has been done. We
do not live in the expectation of a great evening, but rather
in the expectation of a morning which the Apocalypse has
told us will be all light—and the author of a Negro spiritual
is correct: "Good God, what a morning it will be!" Without
this eschatology, nothing has any sense in the Christian life,
neither prayer, nor the communion of saints, nor the Church,
nor combat for justice and charity, nor renunciation of self.[9]
And it is by means of a twofold liberation that the sacraments bring salvation to our history.

THE SACRAMENTS AND THE
UNITY OF OUR EXISTENCE

It is quite well to be in shape for a project; but so long as we remain alone in front of our project, we do not know what to do. Living in time is living in the fractioned, the fragmentary, and the discontinuous. There is no activity that can exhaust all of our resources, no more than a single child can express all of paternity's possibility, nor a single painting exhaust the creative power of an artist. There is no human activity that absorbs all of our possibilities; we need an infinity of them which inevitably succeed each other, one after the other. This sums up the drama of human happiness on earth: we can always want something else. We cannot find rest on the level of our activity and we learn this very quickly as soon as we try to evade it. Man cannot find his unity in the unfolding of his history, no more than the meaning of the history of men reveals itself merely on the level of events. The situation is rather like a calculating machine, because no matter how far it goes in rapidity and verification, it cannot have the necessary regression to read the results. There is no remedy.

What the sacraments bring us is this possibility to confront ourselves everyday with the result of our life. They permit us to recover the present instant, the task of the moment —for example, birth in Baptism, a certain fault or a certain sin in Penance, a certain illness in the Anointing of the Sick, a certain day in the Eucharist—with the ultimate purpose of our life, definitive union with God and formation of the total Body of Christ. They oblige us to refer to something beyond history which nevertheless is not foreign to history.[10] Every morning, the priest is contemporary with the Last Supper, the Cross, and the Resurrection. Each penitent, each sick person, each newly confirmed, is really the contemporary of Easter and Pentecost.

The sacraments have the power to recapitulate our life; they attach us to a reality which surpasses the fragmenting of our psychology. This has been called the threefold dimension of the sacraments.[11] They hold together the present, past, and future. Facing the past, they reanimate for us the source of all life and of all salvation: they make present the power of the Passion of Christ without there occurring two separate acts. The Mass or absolution in the sacrament of Penance does not re-begin the Last Supper or the Redemption. The sacraments do not repeat Christ's acts, but make them present to our life by applying to us the very power of these acts. At ordination, the bishop does not transmit to the priest the priesthood of Christ as we would give someone a gift; rather, he attaches him to the priesthood of Christ. In a sacrament, each Christian participates in the very gesture of the Savior; Christ enables us to perform the act with him. We do not aid our Lord; he does not aid us; but we perform in him what he performed.

"You have been taught that when we were baptised in Christ Jesus we were baptised in his death; in other words, when we were baptised we went into the tomb with him and joined him in death, so that as Christ was raised from the dead by the Father's glory, we too might live a new life. If in union with Christ we have imitated his death, we shall also imitate him in his resurrection. We must realize that our former selves have been crucified with him" (Rom. 6:3-6). And we can rightly think of the inexpressible joy we will have in beatific vision when we can finally see this bond clearly. If we know what happiness between two beings who love each other accompanies their discovery of the bonds of their affections, what will be the great discovery of Christ as one who is greater than one's self! On the doorway of the cathedral of Chartres, it is in looking at God that Adam understands what he is and whose image he is.

But we must go still further. Not only do we become by means of the sacraments contemporaries of a past that is the very source of our salvation, but we become capable of recuperating the past, of retaking and reconstructing our life by giving it a new unity. We know that there is a distance between "me" and my history, between the depths of ourselves and our acts. Our actions commit us; but, once they are performed, they escape us and accumulate behind us and form the chain of our history. And this past can be crushing.

The sacraments continually permit us to transcend this history, and to judge it, and, to a degree, to change its meaning and the value of the whole by means of new acts. This, for example, is the meaning of "satisfaction" in the sacrament of Penance; it is the presence of ever new grace in marital fidelity; it is the permanence of the sacerdotal character beyond every infidelity. The sinner who has been reconciled to God in his person, nevertheless drags behind him in his past a failure towards God, a failure towards love; it is true that at one moment in his history he failed the order of charity which should be reflected in every human undertaking. The event, this sin, remains a fact forever; but by means of the sacraments it can take on another meaning in the entirety of its history, and this by means of new acts repairing the disorder. It is possible for us to restore God's honor, not only in our heart, but in the course of our history which is still being written. It is possible to change the profile of our past acts by means of new compensating acts. This is a marvelous conversion which the sacraments place within our reach! We become capable of much more than a compensation for the past; we become capable of offering to God a life really ordered by love. This is where the reflection we mentioned above concerning healing the past by means of present actions takes on its force. The sacraments do not only remove the sickness from suffering; they go infinitely farther: they transfigure and transvalue what was perversion and evil into an occasion and fruit of divine friendship.

In this way, the sacraments, which permit us to regrasp our past, give meaning to the present and heal it of all emptiness. The present instant, the only center of all faith and of all Christian mysticism, is invested with an infinite dignity and a truly divine power. By means of the present instant, divine friendship acts in our life in the same way as it acted in the life of Jesus.

This is the sacraments' grace, this is their value, eternal life already begun. And their assurance is that if God paid for our destiny with the death of his son, he will not abandon us. "Anyone who does eat my flesh and drink my blood *has* eternal life" (Jn. 6:54). The baptised has only one answer to give to the Church when he is asked at the beginning of his baptism what he is looking for: "eternal life." The future is already there.

There is a real liberation proper to Christianity. By this Christian concept of time and the practice of the sacraments, we are taken out of time's prison as the ancients imagined it, taken out of a universe that is closed in on itself. The Greek idea was certainly very noble, and it consisted of a world called to perfection in which time had no other role than to let things go along toward their accomplishment and to follow it up with a return of the same stages in a necessary cycle so that each person might have time to develop. But this eternal return of time produces a closed world in which man, and finally God also, is imprisoned.

On the contrary, modern science recognizes evolution; it admits that our history accomplishes itself in an irreversible time. We are on the march. Humanity in its entirety is engaged in a progress which we can measure, despite tragic periods of uncertainty. But, science and the imagination of men propose only results to obtain: we need to examine things by touching and feeling them and we like to see the results that indicate our march of progress. But we remain on the horizontal. Under what banner are we on the march? Because it is not easy to decide what we must destroy or construct or what we must keep or abandon in the name of progress.

The great difficulty is to destroy. The cement has become hardened with the passage of time. It takes strong men to break through it; and once the space has been cleared, there will always be the builders, restorers, and decorators. With the best intentions in the world, men consolidate, while time is marching on. There comes a day when the cement requires a battering-ram or even a capsule of dynamite (Alfred Sauvy).

Let us take an example: who feels that he has the right to stop the progress of medicine and research under the pretext that we are prolonging useless and unconscious lives or that we are producing abnormal ones? We are not eager to return to the principles of Hitlerian racism, and yet can we conceal the fact that we are all responsible for the destiny of one more abnormal person?

Where can we find what will order us all to a single end?

What will be the principle strong enough to organize our finalities and not only our fatalities? On what can we base our civilizations so that they may escape death: the appetite to live? organization of the planet? research to increase human well-being? The world is evolving; marvelous tools are in our hands; but where is time leading us?

Between the management of a prison—a marvelously ordered prison, but a prison nevertheless—and the admirably dynamic aspiration toward the indefinite, is situated the newness of Christian time. We are part of a plan, an economy, a project which is not only irreversible, but organized and oriented towards a destination which can be understood by its already present terminus: from now on, salvation is in process in the world, God became man so that man may be God. The "omega" point is not only for later; it is terribly present, and it is called the divine will. It is Another we must take into account, like the bereaved Ezechiel, Jeremiah in his celibacy, David in his sin, Osee in reconciliation, and the Virgin Mary in the Incarnation.

And time, my time, is not only a fatality I endure, but a good I construct day after day in accepting Providence and in embracing a compelling but adorable will, because it is the will of Someone who desires, more than myself, my own fulfillment.

It is true that by means of sin I have the power to break time and to interrupt the destiny of history and its order. It is true that by means of the Incarnation God takes to his account everything old and new and he re-creates this time. It is true that by means of the sacraments each one of us has at his disposal a privileged means to give time its ultimate consequence, but on one condition: that we want to.

There is another liberation: fidelity to the sacraments

works a conversion and creates new attitudes in us; in a word, they dispel fear from our existence. We might cite Simone de Beauvoir who expresses with rare force the human agony in face of the passage of time! Although it is perhaps difficult to suspend one's judgment regarding responsibilities, this agony at least merits being heard.

Oh, the superiority of being alive! . . . In the eyes of those twenty-year-olds, I see myself already dead and mummified. . . .

I can't get around to believing it. When I read in print Simone de Beauvoir, it is a young woman they are telling me about, and who happens to be me. Often in my sleep I dream that in a dream I'm fifty-four. I wake and find I'm only thirty. "What a terrible nightmare I had!" says the young woman who thinks she's awake. Sometimes, too, just before I come back to reality, a giant beast settles on my breast: "It's true! It's my nightmare of being more than fifty that's come true!" How is it that time, which has no form nor substance, can crush me with so huge a weight that I can no longer breathe? How can something that doesn't exist, the future, so implacably calculate its course? My seventy-second birthday is now as close as the Liberation Day that happened yesterday.

To convince myself of this, I have but to stand and face my mirror. . . . I see my face as it was [seen by a passerby], attacked by the pox of time for which there is no cure.

My heart too has been infected by it. I have lost my old power to separate the shadows from the light, to pay the price of the tornadoes and still make sure I had the radiance of clear skies between. My powers of revolt are dimmed now by the imminence of my end and the fatality of the deteriorations that troop before it; but my joys have paled as well. Death is no longer a brutal event in the far distance; it haunts my sleep. Awake, I sense its shadow between the world and me: it has already begun. That is what I had never foreseen: it begins early and it erodes. Perhaps it will finish its task without much pain, everything having been stripped from me so completely that this presence I have so longed to retain, my own, will one day not be present anywhere, not be, and allow itself to be swept away with indifference. One after the other, thread by thread, they have been worn through, the bonds that hold me to this earth, and they are giving way now, or soon will.

Yes, the moment has come to say: Never again! It is not I who am saying good-bye to all those things I once enjoyed, it is they who are leaving me; the mountain paths disdain my feet. Never again shall I collapse, drunk with fatigue, into the smell of hay. Never again shall I slide down through the solitary morning snows. Never again a man. . . . But what hurts more than all these deprivations is never feeling any new desires: they wither before they can be born in this rarefied climate I inhabit now. Once, the days slipped by with no sense of haste. I was going even faster than they, drawn into the future by all my plans. Now the hours are all too short as they whirl me on in the last furious gallop to the tomb. I try not to think: In ten years, in a year. Memories grow thin, myths crack and peel, projects rot in the bud; I am here, and around me circumstances. If this silence is to last, how long it seems, my short future!

And what threats it includes! The only thing that can happen now at the same time new and important is misfortune. Either I shall see Sartre dead, or I shall die before him. It is appalling not to be there to console someone for the pain you cause by leaving him. It is appalling that he should abandon you and then not speak to you again. Unless I am blessed by a most improbable piece of good fortune, one of these fates is to be mine. Sometimes I want to finish it all quickly so as to shorten the dread of waiting.[12]

This is how far we have to go in order to perceive a little the realism of the sacraments. Little by little they teach us

to leave false regrets about the past. Without our even noticing it, our viewpoint changes and we learn that bitterness is
not Christian.

We become more demanding of the present. It is not
simply the material of human work. It belongs to the Body
of Christ which is being constructed. And it is possible for us
to retard this construction when we let ourselves misuse the
present.

Finally, we discover that every temptation to despair in
face of the future, and that all of the despair of men, is
within our power to transfigure into a prayer and a hope
which cannot pass away, by means of the agony in the garden
of olives. We learn the attitude of hope; we lean on Another
who cannot fail us, because he is God.

None of these attitudes in face of the past, present, or
future, escape history. By means of the sacraments, we are
brought to construct our own history on the model of what is
most human in the history of men: the life of Christ. Because
of the sacraments, our past is now constituted by progress and
struggle toward salvation, led by Christ and by Easter continued in the Church.

Our present is Christ's call proposing to us his friendship,
day after day, in every face he puts on for us to recognize him
in his Eucharist and in his poor.

Our future is the glory of Christ and the glory of his Body,
to which we will each be called by name:

Here God lives among men. He will make *his home among
them; they shall be his people,* and he will be their God; his
name is God-with-them . . . *he will wipe away all tears from
their eyes;* there will be no more death, and no more mourning
or sadness. The world of the past has gone (Rev. 21:3–4).

How can we think that the sacraments might be an occasion for escape, when they alone oblige us to waste no time and when they alone bind us to the most extraordinary Incarnation, to him whom nothing human escapes? In allowing us to model our history on a human history, Christ's, the sacraments teach us to love time and to love our history. Not only do they bring all the weight of the divine to bear on the present instant, but they free us from the fear of being alone in the project of our life.

Little by little, the sacraments accustom us to this mystique of substitution and of the present instant—which are two decisive aspects of every truth of the life of faith in a man; and in this way, they cultivate in us God's mildness and patience. "Do little things like great ones for the sake of the majesty of him who does them in us"; there is no other way to charity than this substituting of Christ, his energies, desires, Passion, Easter, for our own. In helping us to work this substitution day by day, the sacraments free us from what is the most terrible in despair: impatience, because we are afraid to be alone. It is not a question of being moral giants, nor of going after God as a mountain-climber attacks a peak. "The only thing that counts is not what human beings want or try to do, but the mercy of God" (Rom. 9:16).

NOTES

1. R. Queneau, *Pierrot mon ami* (Paris: Ed. Gallimard), p. 124.

2. Cf. Gregory of Nyssa, *The Life of Moses,* translated into French by J. Daniélou, *Sources chrétiennes* (Paris, 1955).

3. Cf. E. Gilson's introduction in *Saint Bernard. Un itinéraire de retour à Dieu,* coll. "Chrétiens de tous les temps" (Paris, 1964).

4. We would like to point out two works which analyze this itinerant and progressive aspect of the Christian life: P.-R. Régamey, *Portrait spirituel du chrétien* (Paris: Ed. du Cerf, 1963), and P. Lucien-Marie, *L'impatience de Dieu* (Paris: Ed. du Cerf, 1964).

5. G. Picon, *Panorama des idées contemporaines* (Paris: Ed. Gallimard, 1957), pp. 16–19.

6. Cf. Heidegger, *Les chemins qui ne mènent nulle part* (Paris: Ed. Gallimard, 1962), part II, "L'époque des conceptions du monde," pp. 71 ff. And cf. by the same author, *Qu'est-ce que la métaphysique?* (Paris: Ed. Gallimard, 1951), section II, chapter 5, "L'être et le temps," pp. 168 ff., "Temporalité et historicité."

7. J. Onimus, "Teilhard de Chardin et l'espoir du monde," in *Janus*, n. 4, January 1965, on the sense of history.

8. On the weight of the myth of history, today, cf. P. Emmanuel, *Le goût de l'un*, pp. 108–112: "The supreme question: is man about to turn himself into an insect or a god?" The author shows how the temptation to dissolve oneself in history is an inevitable sickness of the spirit. If we do not want to accept eschatology by a real union with God, we inevitably re-create it on our human horizon: in our work, our family, or city.

9. We have tried to show what is at stake in this truth in two articles published in *La Vie Spirituelle:* "Doit-on être dans l'angoisse en face de la prédestination?", January 1962, pp. 53 ff.; "Nous avançons à reculons. La Providence et notre avenir," March 1962, pp. 305 ff.; "Espérance et prière," December 1959, pp. 506 ff. It is always good to recall the importance of this reflection on eschatology in the ecumenical dialogue. Treating of "Present time in the Bible," Professor Cullmann recently affirmed: "What is new in Jesus with regard to Judaism, is the tension between the 'already' and the 'not yet.' We are in the time of the Holy Spirit, the time of the Church; and this is the basis of all ecumenical dialogue. The Church is the anticipation of the Kingdom, but it is not yet the Kingdom. Between the Catholic Church and the Protestant Churches, who place different accent on the 'not yet' and the 'already,' dialogue can only be fertile."

10. *History is always relative.* Cf. Elsa Triolet, on the nostalgia of every historian and his inability to escape a dead-end on the level of events: "The possibility which the historian has to consider certain

facts—true or false—in their becoming, permits him to take himself for a sage. . . . Every age lives in the context of its times; and the historian's interpretations are also part of the age in which they were written, and are not part of the age in which the interpreted facts happened. The lesser evil would be that the historian limit himself to enumerating the data he possesses, with all the transformations they have undergone up to the time. The march of History augments, deforms, and makes precise its own data. And what does this mean? That we should speak of the Resistance without taking into account its deciphering by the post-Liberation, or Napoleon's victories without Saint-Helena? No answer" (*Le Grand Jamais,* Paris: Ed. Gallimard).

11. Cf. J. M. Tillard, "La triple dimension du signe sacramentel" in the *Nouvelle revue théologique,* March 1961, pp. 225–254. Cl.-J. Geffré, "Les sacrements et le temps," in *La Maison-Dieu,* n. 65, 1961, pp. 96–108, a special number on "Le Christ hier, aujourd'hui, toujours."

12. Reprinted by permission of G. P. Putnam's Sons from *Force of Circumstance* by Simone de Beauvoir. English translation copyright © 1964, 1965 by G. P. Putnam's Sons. Pp. 654–657, *passim.*

4 The Seven Sacraments

If the paschal mystery gathers up the deepest needs of our life (transcendence of distress, fulfillment of self and encounter with others in dialogue, recapitulation of time and victory over death) and if it really answers them, how can we apply its energies to them?

By the sacraments.

Let us begin by examining them before trying to discover the intentions by which God directs them.

The source and the estuary. A man who has seen no more than the source of a river cannot pretend to know the river, anymore than can someone who has only seen its estuary. And a man who would walk the length of this river in one direction, whether it be upstream or downstream, would undoubtedly miss many of its beauties. The same is true of our knowledge of Christ or our comprehension of the sacraments.

With St. John, we have to set out from the source, from God who sent his Son in whom was all life; and we have to discover little by little how this life which was offered to us was light, and how this light was eclipsed by darkness. But we must also follow the inverse movement with the synoptic gospels and retrace the course of human hope. With St. Matthew, we must relive the Jewish people's expectation of a Messiah, and with St. Luke, the pagan peoples' expectation of a saving prophet. All along the history of the Church, Christians have followed this twofold movement: the one that begins with God and awaits the day of wrath and justice, the manifestation of his wisdom and power, and the one that begins with men and awaits the perfect Man, the new Adam who recapitulates humanity. The same is true for the seven sacraments. When we examine them, we place ourselves on the landing-field, because everything that has come from the divine life ends there. But our examination would be insufficient if we did not then ask where these energies of salvation come from and what are the intentions of God's heart.

God admits whom he will, and as he wills, into the society of his life. No prescribed form can ever limit God's gift, in the same way as nothing can ever answer the despair of men except God himself who alone knows why this despair was permitted. In limiting our inquiry to the seven sacraments, we are no more limiting the divine generosity than we are human distress. We are only setting out from that which we know.

If the Church took twelve centuries to begin speaking of *seven* sacraments, it is not because it invented them. It simply began by *living,* by imitating Christ who is the gift of God, God given by God himself to men. In conformity with the Gospel and with the actions of its Savior, it shared the bread and the wine, it proposed to those who came to it that they purify themselves, it forgave, it fought against evil, and it blessed human love. And one day, faced with all the questions that this posed, it solemnly became aware that these were the sacraments; and it stated precisely that they were the best part of man's life and the different ways that Christ has chosen to accompany the existence of each one of us towards its fulfillment. We can no more reduce God's gift and the sharing of Christ's energies to seven more or less magical moments than we can reduce the Incarnation to a few privileged moments in the history of Jesus, though they be transcribed by the gospels. *The entire existence of the Christian is sacramental.* It is this or it is nothing. St. Augustine and St. Bernard were not wrong when they affirmed, for example, that the reading of Holy Scripture, preaching the Word of God, and the washing of feet—that is, taking care of the poor and the brethren—are sacramental gestures.

The Christian mystery is the mystery of God who seeks man, a God who "passes" into the life of man to save him. And in the end, the sacraments are nothing other than the extension into the present time of the energies of God in his search for man. They are nothing other than the ever renewed activity of a saving God. Outside of Christ's intentions which are intentions of salvation, we can understand nothing about the sacraments.[1]

Examining the sacraments does not consist in deciphering some kind of secret code whose meaning is reserved to initiates. No, the things which God has done can be understood in the way in which he did them, and they can speak to us according to the meaning that God has given them. For us then, it is a matter of listening to Christ's intentions through the events and things which are his ambassadors.

We cannot pretend to say everything here, but we will try to suggest what is essential to each sacrament. It is evident that Christ's intentions will always overflow whatever we can express with words. And this is perhaps one of the advantages of the sacraments; they show us that we are powerless to translate everything they can tell us, they make us modest and finally lead us to silence. We should be attentive to the great simplicity of each one of these signs. The sacraments speak by themselves, and their richness is so great that we can never finish scrutinizing them.

In daily practice, a doctor must understand concretely that he cannot treat one part of the human organism without being very careful for the equilibrium of all the rest of the body. The same is true for the sacraments. We cannot dissociate them one from the other, and we cannot understand the sacraments in general, without continually referring to each one among them. This is why the totality of this book concerns all the sacraments, or more exactly, our way of living them religiously, of "practicing" them.

Here, however, we will briefly examine each sacrament in order to know what we are talking about afterwards.

It is possible to follow a number of different schemas to treat the sacraments. We can consider them according to their individual necessity for salvation (and the unfolding in time of this salvation), or we can consider them according to the stages in the constitution of the Christian assembly, or finally, according to their real importance.

In the first case, we would follow a genetic order: Baptism, Confirmation, Penance, etc. which is justified by the progression we will discuss later. In the second case, we would begin with the sacrament of Orders, because without it there would be neither a constituted Church nor a liturgical community; and then would come the sacraments of initiation, and then the Eucharist, and the sacraments of reconciliation.

We prefer to begin here with the Eucharist, because it is the sacrament which gives us, in the richest and fullest way, all of Christ's intentions. After the Eucharist, we will look at the sacraments of reconciliation and healing (Baptism, Confirmation, Penance, Anointing of the Sick), and finally the sacraments of maturity and fruitfulness (Matrimony and Orders).

THE EUCHARIST

"Every time you eat this bread and drink this cup, you are proclaiming the death of the Lord" (I Cor. 11:26). Christ's first intention is that the Covenant be restored in an eternal reconciliation. "This is the blood of the New Covenant poured out for many,"—"this is the body given ('broken' according to some versions of St. Paul's text) for you." Christ's intention is the salvation of the human race accomplished by the offering of his sacrifice. The first announcement of this sacrament is that of a death which "turns back" Adam's sin. The bread and wine are separated, like a body emptied of its blood and like wine poured out in an offertory cup.

Christ's primary intention, the reconciliation of humanity with God, is inseparable from a second movement which is addressed to men rather than to God: the gift of eternal life made to the human race. "I am the living bread which has come down from heaven. Anyone who eats this bread will live forever; and the bread that I shall give is my flesh, for the life of the world" (Jn. 6:61). The body and blood of Christ are handed over, broken, pierced by the lance which opens the source of eternal life. And we are joined to the fruits of salvation.

But now Christ has come, as the high priest of all the blessings which were to come. He has entered the sanctuary once and for all, taking with him not the blood of goats and bull-calves, but his own blood, having won an eternal redemption for us. He brings a new covenant, as the mediator, only so that the people who were called to an eternal inheritance may actually receive what was promised (Heb. 9:11–15).

Christ's second intention in giving us the Eucharist is to

definitively give us eternal life. The pledge and the deposit
are now given to us in the Eucharist.

The sacrifice and offering of Christ are made present to
us around a table, by the means of nourishment. And this is
another of Christ's intentions.

The Eucharist accomplishes in a special way what all of
the other sacraments realize: our life is taken over by the life
of God; we assimilate God, his body, blood, soul and divinity, in order to be assimilated by him. "If you do not eat the
flesh of the Son of Man and drink his blood, you will not
have life in you" (Jn. 6:53). In receiving his body, we receive Christ's entire life. We eat God. We become members
of Christ; we are attracted to him and invested with his life
which itself is filled by his divinity. The Curé d'Ars was correct to say, "If we really understood this mystery, we would
die." It is the consummation of God's ineffable union with
man; God accomplishes what no human love can. We do not
have the right to list these truths under the name of "mysticism" nor to imagine that the only persons concerned are
those who are either sufficiently sick or previously disposed
to think about the supernatural. Chapter six of St. John is
explicit enough on this: Christ is not addressing himself to
a few men who have been touched with a special charism or
a sickness, to the exclusion of normal people, but to everyone; and his intentions belong to the essence of Christian
faith. The Apostles felt a certain uneasiness in face of the
idea of such an absolute sharing of God's life. For us as for
them, it is a threshold of faith. God made himself our food
and realized in this way the ultimate desire of love, which is
to become only one.

But we must immediately add that when two living beings
meet each other, it is the stronger who assimilates the other;
and we must conclude with St. Augustine, from the texts of

St. John and St. Paul, that finally it is we who become God's food and who become God. "I am the food of the great. Become great and you will eat me. But it is not you who will change me into you, as you do food in your body; it is I who will change you into me" (St. Augustine). This idea is so important for our understanding of the sacraments and so decisive for our conversion that we will spend more time on it later.

Between the Lord and us, it is he who is living, he who is the stronger and the more active; it is we who eat and grow, but it is he who assimilates us to him, including our every activity, spiritually and carnally, one sole being, one sole living being with him. And this in such a way that, by means of the Eucharist, our passage from the first Adam to the second is realized; it is the passage from a terrestrial condition to a heavenly and, in a way, divine condition.

It is not for nothing that Christ chose to be given to us as food. We will never stop rejoicing at this unity we have found and this resurrection that has begun. By means of the bread, the symbol of strength, and the wine, the symbol of joy, we are assimilated to the eternal Christ who lives by his Father.

"The blessing-cup that we bless is a communion with the blood of Christ, and the bread that we break is a communion with the body of Christ. The fact that there is only one loaf means that, though there are many of us, we form a single body because we all have a share in this one loaf" (I Cor. 10:16–17). There can be no better announcement of the divine life than this body and blood of Christ. This life circulates through the members of a "mystical" body, as blood circulates in a living being. And the wine, taken from the vine where all the branches make only one, living by means of the same sap, is a symbol of the blood.

Christ's last act before his sacrifice—and, indeed, it is part
of the sacrifice—was to gather his friends together at a meal,
the Last Supper. He invites us to eat together. It is only at
the moment when friendship is made visible in the meal,
which is the strongest symbol men have for their common
joy, that God gives his life. God did not want us to commune
only with him and with his life; he wanted us to become
identical with Christ by forming one single body and, in this
way, communing "with" others.

St. Paul calls communion the fact that we are his body. What is
the bread? The body of Christ. And what do those who participate become? The body of Christ. Not many bodies, but one
single body. In the same way as one single loaf of bread is composed of many grains, and the grains are no longer apparent
even though they remain, and because of their union their difference disappears, so also we are united one with the other and
all of us with Christ. Because one person is not nourished with
one body and another person with another body; but we are all
nourished with the same body (St. John Chrysostom).

When we come to understand the deeply communal significance of the meal, we discover how this symbol comple-
ments the symbol of food. But, on the other hand, we must
never forget that this meal is a body offered up in sacrifice.

A SHORT SCRIPTURAL GUIDE
TO THE EUCHARIST

1. The institution and primitive celebration
   of the Eucharist.
Four texts referring to the institution of the Eucharist:

Mt. 26:26–29; Mk. 14:22–25; Lk. 22:15–20; I Cor. 11:23–25.

The Eucharist was instituted during the course of a paschal meal prepared by two disciples: Mk. 14:12–16; Lk. 22:7–13; Mt. 26:17–19.

The Eucharist transforms an ordinary meal into the supper of the Lord: I Cor. 11:20–34.

In the primitive Church, the Eucharist was celebrated only weekly: Acts 20:7–11.

2. *The sacrament of a sacrifice.*

This Body and Blood are poured out "for you" and "for many": Lk. 22:19–20; Mk. 14:24.

This Body is given for "the remission of sins": Mt. 26:27.

On the cross, "blood and water" flowed from Jesus' side: Jn. 19:34.

Christ enclosed the richness of this sacrifice in nutriments.

In repeating this gesture, Christians "announce the death of the Lord": I Cor. 11:26.

They do it "in his memory": I Cor. 11:24–25; Lk. 22:19.

They recall his redemptive act to God's memory: Acts 10:4; 10:31. Cf. Lev. 2:2, 9–16; 24:7; Num. 10:9–10; Sir. 50:16.

They participate in God's love by receiving the Body of the Lord in communion, and in him with all his members: I Cor. 10:14–22.

3. *The sacrament of a nourishment.*

a) From figures to reality.

God communicates life to his people by means of manna and quail: Ex. 16:2–21, and by means of water that burst from the rock at Horeb: Ex. 17:1–6; Num. 20:1–11; Ps. 78:19–29.

b) The Lord's Supper.

By his Word, Jesus is "the Bread of life": Jn. 6:26–51.

Jesus gives his flesh and blood to eat and drink; "this is my flesh for the life of the world": Jn. 6:51–58.

This bread of life, the true bread from heaven, is given to us by the father: Jn. 6:30–33.

"Anyone who eats my flesh and drinks my blood has eternal life, and I shall raise him up on the last day": Jn. 6:53–58.

*4. The sacrament of the present
and future Kingdom.*

The Eucharist announces the future Kingdom: Lk. 22:-14–16.

The Kingdom of God is compared to a feast: Mt. 8:11–12; Lk. 14:15–24; Mk. 14:25; Mt. 22:2–10.

Intimacy with Christ is a prelude to the messianic feast: Rev. 3:20–21; Lk. 22:29–30.

The death of Christ opens onto the true way: Rom. 6:8–10.

It is the eschatological age of future goods: Heb. 10:1; Col. 2:17.

This sacrifice has been made "once and for all": Heb. 7:26–27; I Pet. 3:18.

The new covenant replaces the old covenant: Heb. 8:3; Heb. 12:24.

The new covenant obtains "the eternal inheritance": Heb. 9:15.

Christ has acquired for us an eternal redemption: Heb. 9:12.

He is "living forever to intercede for us": Heb. 7:25.

The Eucharist gives the believer physical contact with Christ in all the reality of his new, resurrected, "spiritual" being: Jn. 6:63.

BAPTISM

The greater a work is, the more effort it demands from the person accomplishing it. A work exists only in proportion to what it costs. Every birth involves a risk of death for the one giving life. We cost the death of the Son of God. Such is the measure of our dignity, and the Church tells us that the child who has just been baptized is looked upon by God as if he personally had lived the passion of Christ.[2]

If tomorrow it were announced to humanity that a cure has finally been found for every type of cancer, what great hope this would bring! But by means of Baptism, the Church tells us that we are definitively freed from every evil and from every death. This is the reality proposed to each one of us, and it is impossible to appreciate.

Nothing is changed externally; but another dimension, an infinite one, is offered to man, and everything in him is modified. If he remains faithful, he will soon discover it, just as the man who has lived in darkness is aroused to new life when the light appears. We can turn off the light, but we can never forget it.

This light is Christ. And so, man is not alone; he is offered the opportunity to do everything in company with another. He has entered a new body, the Body of Christ. And this is so real a body that he has entered the Church.

Because of sin, the door between God and man is closed and access to God's life is impossible without redemption. That he be the saving sacrifice which opens the door to everyone who will follow, is the new intention of Christ's Passover.

Christ's blood became the symbol of this saving sacrifice. And all those who are marked with this blood see the door open. "You have been taught that when we were baptized in Christ Jesus we were baptized in his death. You too must consider yourselves to be dead to sin but alive for God in Christ Jesus" (Rom. 6:3, 11). The stain of sin is the obstacle to be removed. We can therefore also say of Baptism that the blood of Christ cleanses man of his sin: "Though your sins are like scarlet, they shall be as white as snow; though they are red as crimson, they shall be like wool" (Is. 1:18). To "baptize" means to soak or drench something; and in this we see Baptism symbolized as a bath in the blood of Christ. We can bathe in the blood which Christ shed during his Passion. We know from now on that there is something stronger than the stain of evil; the water of Baptism really can purify us of every sin. The water of purification is also the water which gives life.

He brought me back to the entrance of the Temple, where a stream came out from under the Temple threshold and flowed eastward, since the Temple faced east. The water flowed from under the right side of the Temple, out of the altar. He took me out by the north gate and led me right round outside as far as the outer east gate where the water flowed out on the right-hand side. The man went to the east holding his measuring-line and measured off a thousand cubits; he then made me wade across the stream; the water reached my ankles. He measured off another thousand and made me wade across the stream again; the water reached my knees. He measured off another thousand and made me wade across again; the water reached my waist. He measured off another thousand; it was now a river which I could not cross; the stream had swollen and was now deep water, a river impossible to cross. He then said, "Do you see, son of man?" He took me further, then brought me back to the bank of the river. When I got back, there were many trees on each bank of the river. He said, ". . . Wherever the river flows, all living creatures teeming in it will live. . . . Along the river, on either bank, will grow every kind of fruit tree with leaves that never wither and fruit that never fails; they will bear new fruit every month, because this water comes from the sanctuary. And their fruit will be good to eat and the leaves medicinal" (Ez. 47:1–7, 9, 12).

"Do you see, son of man?" We can never finish seeing the superabundance of life which Baptism brings us. The river flows ever more rapidly, as at the time of high tide. The entire earth is made fruitful by this river and, paradoxically, to point out how completely this mystery surpasses us, the farther man goes, the deeper the water is.

We might summarize the symbolic sequence of Baptism in this way: we are called to take off the stained clothing of the old man in order to enter the regenerative water, and we come out after having put on the new life, after having put on Christ. Then, wearing the nuptial robe, we can enter the banquet-hall. As we are told at the end of the baptismal ceremony, "Keep this clothing without stain . . . until the tribunal of God." "All baptized in Christ, you have all clothed yourselves in Christ" (Gal. 3:27).

Besides being the departure-point, birth of new life, pardon, and superabundance of life, Baptism is also a sign of the resurrection. "If in union with Christ we have imitated his death, we shall also imitate him in his resurrection" (Rom. 6:5). Baptism is the sacrament of regeneration; it is the sacrament of the principle of life which will be our definitive resurrection, and this is the power of the Passion and Christ's intention which he transmits to us.

In itself, the Eucharist is more important than Baptism because it is Christ himself present, but Baptism signals the first application of the powers of Christ's Passion in our personal history. Although we can never be baptized over again, any more than we can be born over again, Baptism is nevertheless repeated under another form by means of Penance which continues this power of the Passion in our life to erase sin.

A SHORT SCRIPTURAL GUIDE TO BAPTISM

1. The Baptism of Jesus.

John the Baptist preaches a baptism of repentance at the Jordan: Mt. 3:5–11; Jn. 1:26.

Jesus, baptized by John, is proclaimed the "Son of God": Mt. 3:13–17; Jn. 1:31–34.

Jesus' baptism announces and prepares his baptism "in death" Lk. 12:50; Mk. 10:38.

This baptism is crowned by the descent of the holy Spirit: Mt. 3:16; Mk. 1:10.

Jesus' baptism announces Pentecost which will inaugurate baptism in the Spirit for the Church: Acts 1:5.

"Can you be baptized with the baptism with which I must be baptized?": Mk. 10:38–40; Lk. 12:50.

2. The Baptism of the Christian.
a) Baptism gives salvation.

"He who believes and is baptized will be saved": Mk. 16:15–16.

"Go therefore, and make disciples of all nations; baptize them in the name of the Father and of the Son and of the Holy Spirit": Mt. 28:19.

b) Baptism introduces us into the Body of Christ.

By means of Baptism, "we have become one being with Christ: Acts 2:38–41; Rom. 6:5; Gal. 3:27; Col. 2:12.

"There are no more distinctions between Jew and Greek, slave and freeman, but all are one in Christ Jesus" and filled with one Spirit: Gal. 3:28; I Cor. 12:13; Col. 3:9–11.

c) And for this, it purifies.

Baptism is a purification:—individual: I Cor. 6:11;—communal and ecclesial: Eph. 5:26–27.

Baptism is a new birth in water and the Spirit: Jn. 3:5; Tit. 3:5.

This baptism "of water and the Spirit" depends on the mystery of the cross by which the Spirit will be given: Jn. 3:5–16.

This bath of regeneration makes the baptized the "child of God": I Jn. 3:1.

Baptism is a new "circumcision": Col. 2:11–12.

It is a "character" imprinted forever: Eph. 4:30; 1:13; II Cor. 1:22.

It is an "illumination": Eph. 5:8–14; Heb. 6:4.

d) In order to make us live in the company of God, Father, Son, and Holy Spirit.

By means of Baptism, the Christian becomes: the "temple of the Spirit": I Cor. 6:19; an adopted child of the Father: Gal. 4:5–7; a brother and "coheir with Christ": Rom. 8:15–17.

The Spirit reveals the Father to him: Tit. 3:5–6.

The Spirit given at Baptism is the Spirit of the resurrected Christ, the "power" which the Lord has received: Acts 2:33.

3. Conversion, faith, and Baptism.

Baptism supposes our confession of faith: Acts 16:30–33.

The faith of the father of the family has value for the entire family: Acts 10:47; 16:33.

The faith of Baptism involves a total conversion, a total giving to Christ who transforms all our life: I Pet. 3:20–21; II Cor. 5:17.

The baptized person is united to other baptized persons in the very unity of Christ and his glorified Body: Gal. 3:25–28; Rom. 13:14.

4. A new life.

Baptism is the condition for entrance into the Kingdom of God: Jn. 3:5.

It is the necessary means for salvation: Mk. 16:16; Jn. 3:3–8; Acts 2:38.

It is entrance into a dynamic state: Rom. 6:12–14.

Baptism symbolizes and realizes participation in the death and resurrection of Christ: the baptized is "plunged" into the death of Christ and buried with him, to rise with him in a new life: Rom. 6:3–4; Col. 2:12; Col. 3:1–11.

It is therefore a paschal sacrament, a communion with Christ's Passover: Rom. 6:4–11; Phil. 3:10–11.

The baptized person lives by the life of Christ: Gal. 2:20.

He undergoes a radical transformation; he puts off the "old man to put on the new man": Gal. 3:27; Col. 3:9–10; Eph. 4:22–24.

The old creature becomes the "new creature": Gal. 6:14–16; II Cor. 5:16–21. (Cf. Ezechiel: the water, the spirit, and the renewal of man: Ez. 36:25–27.)

CONFIRMATION

Christ's Passion is a supreme act of power, the power of the love of the Son of God made man for his Father, and the ultimate witness to this love. Christ acquired the right to communicate to us the same power and the same love, as well as the power to enable us to witness in our turn, without failing, "right to the end." Our Lord said to St. Peter, "Where I am going, you cannot now follow. . . ." But, by the power of the Passion, Peter also will go all the way to crucifixion.

Christ's energy therefore has the power of confirming the children of God, as the Apostles were confirmed on the day of Pentecost. This power of confirmation is a fruit not only of the Word of God, but also of the Passion and Resurrection. Before Christ's Passover, the Apostles were in a quasi-childish state, weak in faith. Con-firmation is opposed to in-firmity. Before the Passion, the Apostles had chased out demons, but this nevertheless did not prevent them from becoming frightened and fleeing, and Peter denied his master. "Simon, Simon! . . . I have prayed for you that your faith may not fail, and once you have recovered, you in turn must strengthen your brothers" (Lk. 22:32).

After having given his body as sacrifice and food, Christ gave to his faithful his Spirit which is breath and fire, the image of violence, totality, and the liberty of love. A special fruit of the Passion is this strength in faith and love all the way to imitating Christ on his way to Calvary, which involves fighting evil and the devil. This fight against the weight of evil in our life is an effect of confirmation. "For it is not against human enemies that we have to struggle, but against the Sovereignties and the Powers who originate the darkness in this world, the spiritual army of evil in the heavens" (Eph. 6:12).

The Spirit of God which is charity will not leave us be until we have consummated all the dynamism of our life in charity, "because the love of Christ presses us." And the Spirit pushes us to construct the Church: "he is the living stone, rejected by men but chosen by God and precious to him; set yourselves close to him so that you too, the holy priesthood that offers the spiritual sacrifices which Jesus Christ has made acceptable to God, may be living stones making a spiritual house" (I Pet. 2:4-5). The first thing that happens to a stone, before it supports others, is to be trimmed to its proper measure. Our activity must be adjusted so that it be really a service to others and not the sometimes illusory satisfaction of social responsibilities. By means of Confirmation, the Spirit seeks to obtain this adjustment in us.

Confirmation is not only the sacrament of a mandate towards other persons; it engages the entire dynamism of man and his activity, and it may therefore commit him to every kind of purification (if water does not suffice, a breath; and if a breath does not suffice, fire) to find his place and accomplish the role—if his liberty consents to it—reserved for him in the definitive plan for the world's salvation.

A SHORT SCRIPTURAL GUIDE
TO CONFIRMATION

1. The Spirit is sent by Jesus.

"Unless a man is born through water and the Spirit, he cannot enter the Kingdom of God": Jn. 3:3–8.

"From the breast of the man who believes in me, shall flow fountains of living water": Jn. 7:37–39.

"The heavenly Father will give the Holy Spirit to those who ask Him": Lk. 11:13.

The Father "will send you another Advocate to be with you": Jn. 14:13–17.

The Spirit "confirms" Baptism: Acts 1:4–8.

Among the early Christians, the coming of the Spirit was indissolubly linked to Baptism: Acts 10:44–47; this is why the imposition of hands immediately followed Baptism: Acts 19:1–7; Acts 8:14–16; Heb. 6:2.

2. The gifts of the Spirit.

The Spirit enables the disciples to understand Jesus' words and actions: "He will teach you everything and remind you of all I have said to you": Jn. 14:16–26.

"He will lead you to the complete truth": Jn. 16:12–15.

In the Spirit, there is no gift we lack: I Cor. 1:7; Gal. 5:22–25.

The Spirit fills us with joy: Acts 13:52.

The Spirit enables us to know "the secrets of God": I Cor. 2:10–12.

The gifts of the Spirit are varied: I Cor. 12:4–11.

We still have only "the pledge" and "the first-fruits of the Spirit"; it is a life that is given to us in battle: II Cor. 1:21–22; Rom. 8:23; II Cor. 5:5.

We become "participators" in the Holy Spirit: Heb. 6:4.

"The oil of unction remains on us": I Jn. 2:27.

It gives us the sense of truth and teaches us everything: I Jn. 2:20.

3. The Spirit enables us, in the image
of Christ, to bear witness until death.

"The Spirit of truth will be my witness, and you too will be witnesses": Jn. 15:26–27; Acts 1:8; 4:31.

The Spirit will give them strength to confront the world in the name of Jesus: Jn. 16:8–11; Mk. 13:11.

The Spirit "will show the world how wrong it was": Jn. 16:7–11.

The Holy Spirit guides the apostles to announce the word: Acts 16:6–7.

PENANCE

Penance expresses a new intention of Christ's Passover. It permits him who is not yet definitively confirmed, but who has already been reborn, to restore fully the friendship which he has wounded. God proposes to us that we have personal recourse to the blood of Christ. In the Gospel, we see sick persons, Mary Magdalen, and lepers throw themselves at Christ's feet. This is the symbol of our penitence. It is a less radical sacrament than birth to faith, but it is a real "resurrection." Sin is death to the true life but the sinner retains enough faith and strength to go look for his cure. "His belief in the remission of his sins is the decisive crisis by which a man becomes spirit; the man who does not believe in the remission of his sins is not spirit."[3]

This healing of the soul manifests another power of the Passion; the blood of Christ is applied exactly where it is most necessary, where we are the sickest. More than any other sacrament, Penance shows us how we are really cooperators with God; our entire Christian life is the action of two together. In Penance, not only is it we who look for healing, but it is we who are invited to re-create our life exactly where we diminished it. God has not wanted to save us without us. In our healing, he wants us to act like the sick person who must himself rebuild his tissues. Our wound brings us to the sacrament for healing so that, like Naaman the leper, the flesh of our life may again become like that of a newborn infant. Therefore, it is our most hidden miseries, the ones we see the least, which belong to the sacrament of Penance.

Penance is without doubt the sacrament in which our person-to-person encounter with Christ is the most noticeable. It is the only sacrament in which there is no other sign but a human act. There is no need for anything exterior; the sign, the support of the sacrament, is the very act of avowal and recognition of sin. Furthermore, Christ wanted this avowal to be made in front of another human being—"Those whose sins *you* forgive . . ."—to assure us that even though the sin has touched God in person, we also are personally loved and pardoned. It is only in the face of him whom we have wounded that we can discover the depth of our sin. The sinner comes to take refuge in the wound he opened by his sin. He washes himself in the very blood he caused to flow. Not only does God pardon, but he does much more; he has come to weep with the sinner, to take on himself the weight of evil, and to stand among the guilty. The Curé d'Ars was quite correct to repeat, "You have just crucified Jesus Christ and sold your soul; but when you go confess your sins, understand well what you do: we might say that you are going to unnail our Lord."

Finally, we confess our sins in front of someone to signify that God's friendship, restored by pardon, reintegrates us with our brothers and with the entire community of believers. But this does not suffice to explain the bond between the sacrament of Penance and the community of our brothers. There is much more; Penance is one of the privileged occasions for the *reciprocity* which is entirely proper to Christianity, the interaction between what we do to others and what God does to us. When Christ says, "What you have done to the least of my brethren, you have done to me," or "According to the measure by which you measure, will it be measured out to you," or when he invites us to love as he loves, that is, as his Father loves, we are touching on what is perhaps the essential point of Christian conversion: not only "Do not do to others what you do not want them to do to you," but "Do not do to others what you do not want God to do to you."

"Forgive us our trespasses, as we forgive those who trespass against us." When we go to Confession, we are not only re-entering communion with our brothers, but we are expressing our desire to share in God's regard for our brothers.[4]

A SHORT SCRIPTURAL GUIDE
TO PENANCE

1. Like the prophets, Jesus invites
to repentance.

John the Baptist proclaims "a baptism of repentance for the remission of sins": Mk. 1:4–5; Mt. 3:2–6.

"If you are repentant, produce the appropriate fruit. Even now the axe is laid to the roots of the trees, so that any tree which fails to produce good fruit will be cut down and thrown on the fire": Mt. 3:8–10.

Jesus in Galilee: "The Kingdom of God is close at hand. Repent, and believe the good news": Mk. 1:14–15; Mt. 4:17.

Jesus sends the twelve to "preach repentance": Mk. 6:12–13.

"I have not come to call the virtuous, but sinners to repentance": Lk. 5:31–32; Mt. 9:10–13; Mk. 2:15–17; Lk. 15:2.

"Unless you repent, you will all perish": Lk. 13:1–5; Jn. 8:24.

"He who rejects me and refuses my words has his judge already: the word itself that I have spoken will be his judge on the last day": Jn. 12:48.

"Rejoicing in heaven over one repentant sinner": Lk. 15:7–10.

Some are blind and refuse to be converted: Mt. 13:13–15; Jn. 12:40.

The prophets invite to repentance: "If you return, God will take you back": Osee 2:16–17; 6:1–3; 14:2–9; Jer. 31:18–20; Ps. 80:4.

"Shake off all the sins you have committed against me, and make yourselves a new heart": Ez. 18:30–32; Ps. 51.

God invites to repentance and promises pardon: Is. 1:16–19; 54:7–8; Jer. 3:12–13; 4:1–4; 7:21–25.

God pardons the humble: Lk. 18:9–14.

"We have our advocate with the Father, Jesus Christ who is just": I Jn.2:1–2.

2. *No one is without sin.*

"I am a man of unclean lips": Is. 6:5–7.

"Can man be in the right against God?": Job 9.

"If there is one of you who has not sinned, let him be the first to throw a stone": Jn. 8:7–9.

"Leave me, Lord; I am a sinful man": Lk. 5:8.

"If we say we have no sin in us, we are deceiving ourselves": I Jn. 1:8–10.

"The man who thinks he is safe must be careful he does not fall. You can trust God not to let you be tried beyond your strength": I Cor. 10:12–13.

"Everybody who does wrong hates the light": Jn. 3:19–21.

"Everyone who commits sin is a slave": Jn. 8:31–36; Rom. 6:17–19.

Sin is also a debt: Mt. 6:12–15; 18:21–25; Mk. 11:25.

Woe to the towns that have not done penance: Mt. 11:20–24; Lk. 10:13–15.

3. *Jesus himself remits sins.*

Jesus forgives the sins of the sinful woman: Lk. 7:36–50; her sins were forgiven "or she would not have shown such great love": Lk. 7:47–48.

The adulteress: Jn. 8:3–11.

Zachaeus: Lk. 19:1–10.

Jesus reveals the Father's joy when he forgives, because it is primarily he, the Father, who is freed by the pardon: he can once again love and be loved by his prodigal son: Lk. 15:11–32.

Jesus vindicates this absolutely divine power of remitting sins: Mk. 2:5–12; Mt. 9:1–8; Lk. 5:20–26.

The good thief is admitted into paradise: Lk. 23:39–43.

4. A reciprocal attitude: to do for others what God has done for us.

"The Lord has forgiven you; now you must do the same": Col. 3:13; Mt. 6:14–15.

"How often must I forgive my brother?": Mt. 18:21–22; Lk. 17:3–4.

The unforgiving debtor: Mt 18:23–35.

"The amount you measure out is the amount you will be given back": Lk. 6:38; Mt. 7:2; Mk. 4:24.

"If you remember that your brother has something against you": Mt. 5:23–24.

"Father, forgive them; they do not know what they are doing": Lk. 23:34.

"Forgive us our debts, as we have forgiven those who are in debt to us": Mt. 6:12; Lk. 11:4.

5. The Church can forgive sins.

Jesus transmits to the Church the power to forgive sins: Mt. 16:19.

Jesus promises the apostles participation in this power: Mt. 18:18.

The apostles, when they have received this power, will sit as judges: Mt. 19:28.

On the evening of Easter, the resurrected Jesus institutes this mission of mercy and sacred power: Jn. 20:21–23.

"In his name, repentance for the forgiveness of sins is preached to all the nations": Lk. 24:47–48.

"God gave us the work of handing on this reconciliation": II Cor. 5:18.

6. *From the time of the apostolic Church,*
   the apostles exercise this power.

St. Paul and the Corinthian guilty of incest: I Cor. 5:1–3.

St. John perhaps faced with a similar case: II Jn. 10:11.

"You too must consider yourselves to be dead to sin but alive for God in Christ Jesus": Rom. 6:8–10.

"You must give up your old way of life; you must put aside your old self, so that you can put on the new self": Eph. 4:22–23.

"Offer yourselves to God, and consider yourselves dead men brought back to life; and then sin will no longer dominate your life": Rom. 6:13–14.

"However great the number of sins committed, grace was even greater": Rom. 5:20.

ANOINTING OF THE SICK

Whatever name we give it, we cannot understand the Christian meaning of this sacrament unless we inquire into Christ's intentions concerning it. The Anointing of the Sick manifests and renders magnificently present two aspects of the Passover. It is like a corporeal echoing of the Passion and Resurrection in our life, with a twofold paradoxical effect:

to avoid death and, at the same time, to make death easier.

The first effect of the Anointing of the Sick is an effect of resurrection; it retards death until the hour desired by God, that is, it mobilizes all the forces of cure against physical collapse.

We should not think that the second effect is contrary to the first. Making death easier is also a consequence of the Passion and Resurrection. Christ comes to give us the power of curing ourselves of *the* fundamental sickness in our life, above and beyond sicknesses of the body, the sickness of the soul: fear, agony in face of the unknown and dissolution. Christ comes to give our death the character of the Resurrection.

To really have a correct notion of the Anointing of the Sick, we must always regard it as the prolongation of the sacraments of Penance and Confirmation. In this way we can see its twofold aspect: with regard to Penance, the remission of sins; with regard to Confirmation, the final strength and capacity for death and resurrection. These two aspects are exemplified very well in the "unction" which is an image of the mildness of God who wants to remove all of the obstacles which sin has accumulated in our life, at the heart of our physical collapse and death, so that we can undergo it not only as a necessity, but make it a free act and entrance to the Resurrection.

A SHORT SCRIPTURAL GUIDE TO ANOINTING OF THE SICK

1. Christ cures the sick.

Christ is the good Samaritan who tends our wounds: Lk. 10:34.

He casts out demons and cures the sick, because he is the "Servant of Yahweh" who bears and removes our illnesses: Mt. 8:16–17; cf. Is. 53:4.

He cures the centurion's servant: Mt. 8:5–13; Lk. 7:1–10; Jn. 4:46–53.

He cures the paralytic: Mt. 9:1–8; Mk. 2:1–12; Lk. 5:17–26.

"The man you love is ill. . . . This sickness will end, not in death but in God's glory": Jn. 11:3–4.

"Your faith deserves it, so let this be done for you": Mt. 9:27–30.

Jesus proclaimed the Good News and cured every sickness: Mt. 11:4–5; Lk. 7:21–22.

2. The disciples receive the power to heal.

The disciples receive "the power to cure all kinds of diseases and sickness": Mt. 10:1; 10:7–8; Lk. 9:1–2; 10:8–9.

"I was sick, and you visited me": Mt. 25:35–36.

3. The disciples anoint the sick with oil.

The disciples anoint the sick and infirm to cure them: Mk. 6:13.

"People came crowding in, bringing with them their sick, and all of them were cured": Acts 5:15–16.

"If one of you is ill, he should send for the elders of the church, and they must anoint him with oil in the name of the Lord and pray over him. The prayer of faith will save the sick man, and the Lord will raise him up again; and if he has committed any sins, he will be forgiven": Jas. 5:13–15.

MATRIMONY

Matrimony existed before the Passion; it is a reality anterior to the New Law. "It is not good that man should be alone" (Gen. 2:18). Besides the supernatural aspect of this sacrament, the natural aspect is so real that the Church holds a marriage between two unbelievers to be valid. This is why, even before we refer to it as an intention of Christ's Passover, marriage is a natural sign of man's supernatural destiny, and much more deeply so than we might imagine. It is one of the privileged signs of God's intimate life and of the very mystery of the Trinity. It is one of the few terrestrial realities which can give us a presentiment of what it means to share one life between many persons and to commune in one common existence.

This mystery of the human couple is such that it permits us to rise to the mystery of the threefold holy God: two Persons, Father and Son, who are "one," this "one," their reciprocal love, having the same force and quality of a Person, the Holy Spirit. This is the first value of the sacrament of Matrimony: the family is truly a sign of God's life.

When men notice that Christians do not take marriage lightly, doesn't this make them suspect that the union of man and woman infinitely surpasses what human words can express? We know well that every time it is a question of love, human words find themselves quite inadequate. There is only one love. And the shortest way from one heart to another passes through the heart of God.

"Husbands should love their wives just as Christ loved the Church and sacrificed himself for her. . . . This mystery has many implications; but I am saying it applies to Christ and the Church" (Eph. 5:25, 32). In a word, St. Paul shows what the sacrament adds to the human reality of marriage: it is the symbol and image of the relationship between God and man.

Christ has established between spouses a mystery analogous to the one by means of which he made the Church his spouse on the cross. Man's supernatural destiny attained its summit only on the day of the Passion. There again, God espoused man. It is at the Passover that God once again declared his love for man. We have the right to speak of the "consummation" of God's love for man; he truly handed over his body for us. Whether we look at it under its aspect of joy in the Eucharist or of suffering in the Passion, it is the same gift of his body. Henceforth, in Christian marriage, between the two spouses, there is the blood of Christ. We must never isolate from each other the two texts by which St. Paul gave us his thought on marriage. There is the Epistle to the Ephesians, but he also wrote about it in the First Epistle to the Corinthians. And we, in Christian matrimony, must courageously maintain everything that St. Paul was charged to say of Christ's intentions: on one hand, that there exists between God and us the equivalent of what exists between a husband and a wife, the same mystery of exclusiveness, faithfulness, patience, and generosity; at the same time that, if the union between Christ and humanity was realized by means of the Passion and cross, the same is true for the union between a husband and a wife, and if the union between Christ and humanity continues and ends up in beatitude, the union between husband and wife is in the same way made to be consummated in happiness. All of this produces under our very eyes one of the most real, most powerful, and at the same time most fragile signs there is of the union between man and God; it is a conjugal union which is consummated on earth only in the Passion and which is completed only in beatitude.

A SHORT SCRIPTURAL GUIDE
TO MATRIMONY

1. Matrimony is created by God.
"It is not good that man should be alone": Gen. 2:18.
Man and woman become "one body": Gen. 2:24.
Fertility is a permanent, divine gift: Gen. 4:1; Gen. 4:25–26; Mt. 19:4–6.

2. Conjugal fidelity.
The Old Testament speaks of:
homes united by a deep love: I Sam. 1:8;
fidelities which freely last beyond death: Jdt. 8:2–8; 16:22;
praises for conjugal stability: Sir. 26:1–4; 26:9–12; Gen. 38:24; Lev. 20:10; Deut. 22:22;
God hates repudiation: Mal. 2:14–16.

3. The Old Testament's religious
ideal of marriage.
The holiness of marriage is sanctioned by precepts given by God: Lev. 18.
The home is prepared by God: Tob. 3:16.
The home is founded under God's vision, in faith and prayer and mutual love: Tob. 8:6.
The home is safeguarded by daily faithfulness to the Law: Tob. 14:1; 14:8–13.

4. The New Law.

Jesus affirms the absolute character of marriage and its indissolubility: Mt. 19:1–9; Mk. 10:1–12; Eph. 5:22–24.

Jesus condemns adultery: Mk. 10:11–12, 19; Mt. 5:27–32; Lk. 16:18; I Cor. 7:10–11.

The disciples are frightened by the rigor of the new law: Mt. 19:10.

This rigor does not exclude Christ's mercy towards offenders: Lk. 7:37–50; Jn. 4:16–19; 8:3–11; Mt. 21:31–32.

His forgiveness emphasizes the value of the betrayed ideal: Jn. 8:11.

5. The sacrament of Matrimony.

Jesus gives matrimony a new foundation; by means of the new covenant which he establishes with his own blood, he himself becomes the spouse of the Church: Mt. 26:28.

This is why matrimony is a "great mystery" with regard to Christ and the Church: Eph. 5:32.

Christ's redemptive love for the Church is in this way the living rule which spouses should imitate; the grace of salvation reaches their love in assigning its ideal: Eph. 5:21–33.

Human sexuality, whose normal exigencies must be prudently appreciated, is assumed into a holy reality which transfigures it: I Cor. 7:1–7.

HOLY ORDERS

People must think of us as Christ's servants, stewards entrusted with the mysteries of God. What is expected of stewards is that each one should be found worthy of his trust (I Cor. 4:1–2). It is all God's work. It was God who reconciled us to himself through Christ and gave us the work of handing on this reconciliation. So we are ambassadors for Christ; it is as though God were appealing through us, and the appeal that we make in Christ's name is: be reconciled to God (II Cor. 5:18, 20).

How can we show someone the respect and dignity we want to give him better than by establishing him as the source of his own destiny. Isn't this Christ's intention in instituting the priesthood? This is one of the most important keys to all the sacraments: God, in his love, wanted to show man such a respect that he judged him capable, with the help of the sacraments, of being the source and principle of his own supernatural destiny. Man shares with Christ the dignity of being at the source of his own salvation; and this enables us to understand the intention of Christ which is particularly present in the sacrament of Holy Orders.

Love forbade God to remain alone. We can refer this truth to Christ's Passover: he does not want to be alone, neither at the Last Supper, nor on the cross, nor when he rises in order to give his life to the world. He wanted the realization of the paschal mystery in time and space to be accomplished through other mediators: priests, servants, responsible with Christ for his people and his Body. When the bishop imposes his hands at ordination—and this is the principal symbol of the sacrament—it is at the same time the sign that Christ takes possession of this person entirely and gives him his power.

This contains a particular intention of Christ. He wanted a perpetual presence of his Passion and Resurrection to exist in the Eucharist. But he wanted this to come about through

the mediation of certain chosen men. In this sense, the priesthood is a consummation of taking hold of the Kingdom,
which occurs for every layman in Baptism and Confirmation.

In every Mass, the priest renews the same offering of his
Body which Christ made on Holy Thursday. In the confessional, and when he baptizes, and in every priestly gesture,
the priest performs the same act of saving the world which
was accomplished on the cross and the same act of liberation
from death and sin by means of the Resurrection. Christ's
intention in the sacrament of Orders is the assimilation of
the priest to himself in carrying out the saving act. Thus,
through Christ, the priest becomes the bearer of the word
which saves and converts by transmitting faith; he can complete the Passion in his body, and be associated with this
power of Christ and say "this is my body" in union with his
own death. In a word, he is responsible for the bread of the
Word and the bread of the Sacrifice, by progressively identifying himself with it.[5]

A SHORT SCRIPTURAL GUIDE
TO ORDERS

1. The priesthood is an institution of Christ.

Christ confers his mission on the twelve: Mt. 10:1–42;
28:16–20; Mk. 6:7–13; Lk. 9:1–6.

He transmits to them some of his powers: Mt. 10:5–8;
18:18; Jn. 20:22–23.

He prepares them for the service of the word: Jn. 17:14–19;
Mk. 9:33–37; Lk. 9:46–48.

"Anyone who listens to you listens to me": Lk. 10:16;
Jn. 13:20.

"I pray for those who through their words will believe in me": Jn. 17:20.

"Consecrate them in the truth": Jn. 17:17–19; 20:21.

"They are in the world. Keep those you have given me true to your name": Jn. 17:11–16; 15:18–21.

Jesus entrusts the sacraments to them: Mt. 28:18–20; 16:19; Mk. 16:15–18.

He entrusts the Eucharist to them: Lk. 22:19; I Cor. 11:24.

2. *The priesthood of Christ.*

Jesus is the mediator-born who manifests God's presence: Jn. 1:14.

Jesus enters the Temple to purify it and acts as master of the house: Jn. 2:13–22; Heb. 3:6. By means of this, Jesus announces that he will open to men access to God: Heb. 9:23.

Jesus, alone, by his sacrifice, penetrates the heavenly sanctuary "beyond the veil": Heb. 6:19–20; 9:11–14.

Jesus is he who opens the way: Jn. 13:1; 14:1–6, 12; Heb. 10:19–22.

Jesus is "the holy one of God" consecrated by his Father to consecrate men: Jn. 6:69; 10:36; 17:17–19; Heb. 10:5–10.

Living for all eternity, Jesus possesses an unchangeable priesthood: Heb. 7:24.

Both true man (Heb. 2:17–18) and true Son of God (Heb. 1:1–4), Jesus is the unique and eternal priest: Heb. 7:25–28.

3. *The priesthood of ordained priests.*

They are "stewards of the mysteries of God," consecrated to serve Christ's priesthood: Jn. 17:17–19; Lk. 12:41–44; I Cor. 4:1–5; II Cor. 5:18–21.

They are "officials of Christ": I Tim. 4:14–16.

This ministerial priesthood is received by the imposition of hands: Acts 14:22–23; 6:1–6; 13:2–3; I Tim. 5:22; II Tim. 1:6.

"I sent you to reap a harvest you had not worked for": Jn. 4:35–38.

Jesus gives them a map for their journey: Mt. 10:9–16; Lk. 9:3–6; 10:2–20.

NOTES

1. *A total revelation.* "And this revelation is total. God has given us his unique Son. He has held nothing back. For this reason, it is useless to look beyond the cross for a mystery of God it does not unveil. There is not in the Absolute a kind of remoter world which keeps other possibilities for surprise. In this sense, the Passion is unsurpassable. It is really the Most High's last word. And it certainly recalls to us the divine incomprehensibility. But if the manner escapes us, the substance of the mystery has been given to us: God is love. So we can say that the Trinity and creation reveal the same fundamental generosity which is beyond every *why*. The cult of Christ's suffering humanity seems to have softened everything by bathing everything in divine tenderness. Creation relaxes in a smile, the smile which on the cross acquiesces to the Father's will and love. It seems that a new breeze passes over the world to raise it up with new ardor. Everyone has received differently from the fullness of Christ crucified. And this inexhaustible fullness is always present. We cannot go beyond it" (S. Breton, *Mystique de la Passion*, Ed. Desclée, 1962, pp. 46–47).

2. Cf. Saint Thomas Aquinas, S.T., III, q. 69, a. 2: "Every baptized person participates in Christ's passion to find in it a remedy so that it is the same as if he had suffered and died himself. . . . In this way, the baptized person is freed from punishment as if he himself had satisfied sufficiently for his sins."

3. S. Kierkegaard, *Journal VIII A* (Paris: Ed. Gallimard), p. 673.

4. *Confession and the others.* If it were just a matter of reestablishing peace between oneself and others, a psychiatrist or lawyer would perhaps often be more capable and more efficacious than a confessor. But it is quite evident here as we evoke the communal dimension of the sacrament of Penance, that it is a matter of much more. It is a matter of accepting Christ's intervention and sharing his strength in the battle against the evil which is in us; it is a matter of permitting God to liberate in us all of the possibilities of pardon and love; and it is a matter of consenting to be in his image. And it is much less difficult than a session with a psychiatrist and much more vast in its intention. When we go to Confession, we meet in a very concrete and real way the unity of the two commandments, because we are asking God to pardon us *as* we pardon others. Might we not say that God's pardon becomes a lure?

5. We are not referring here to contemporary reflections and studies on the foundation of the priesthood and its two aspects of consecration and function.

It seems to us that the problem is sometimes posed equivocally in order to justify a state of life that we would want to change in order to avoid its demands. It seems to us quite difficult to limit the priesthood to the exercise of a "function" without recalling *at the same time* everything which this function supposes and evokes. Therefore, there can be no question of opposing consecration to Christ with functional service of the people of God, because both are distinguished only to be united. Père Carré admirably showed this in his conferences at Notre-Dame de Paris: *Le vrai visage du prêtre* (Paris: Ed. du Cerf, 1959), and *Prêtres et laïcs, apôtres de Jésus-Christ* (1961). Also cf. P. Grelot, *Le ministère de la Nouvelle Alliance,* "Foi vivante" (1967).

5 Why Sacraments?

TO ASSIMILATE GOD

Many of the Jesuits who evangelized New France suffered martyrdom. And it is told how the Iroquois, amazed at their courage and wanting to discover the secret, ate the heart of one of these martyrs after having killed them. This terrible gesture of eating a man's heart in order to assimilate into oneself its secret, corresponds to a deep religious instinct.

Every man has felt this desire *to assimilate the life of another:* all life is constituted by this movement. What does the child do when he discovers other beings and things? Look at him take an object which is new to him: he grasps it, presses it to himself, feels its solidity, and then he puts it to his mouth to taste it. And if it pleases him, he holds it tight against himself, so much so that it is hard to take it out of his hands. He does this with things and also with the persons who surround him.

And what does a person who loves and who suffers from his love do with the person he loves? He tries to discover to what point he has become one with the person he loves. This is our experience, and it can help us to understand God's intention in the sacraments. Nutrition, an act which is both banal and mysterious, places us immediately at the heart of the sacraments.

We too often limit the aim of the sacraments to the merely human broadening of our life. We say that the Eucharist is a daily strength administered like the food which answers the needs of our life, that Baptism is a purification by means of a bath and conforms to human religious customs, that Matrimony is a consecration of what is most profound in love and of the gift of fruitfulness, that Confirmation is the spiritual stabilizing of man's forces for the combat of adult age, etc. *And all of this is insufficient, if we have not understood God's real purpose in giving us the sacraments.* And this purpose surpasses us, even as it remains profoundly human.

Why did God choose gestures that are so human? The answer is a short one: *God gives God to men,* but a gift which is not adapted is not a true gift. And at the same time, a gift which would not surpass us would be uninteresting.

We can often say about any religious gesture, even a non-Christian one, everything we say about the sacraments: it translates by means of a human symbol the desire for union with God. Therefore, how do the sacraments differ from other religious customs?

The sacraments concern much more than union with God in the way that other religious gestures propose it. In the sacraments, we ourselves repeat divine acts and can be co-operators *in the divine life itself.*

God makes us a proposal and asks for a response. And he makes this proposal in such a way that we receive it *in virtue of a movement as elementary and carnal as the most humble movements of human life:* in eating the Eucharist, we eat the divine life. This is much more than a simple union with God; *it is much more than any kind of prayer.* And yet, it suffices to eat, the most elementary of human realities.

Consummation of union with God, "that they be one . . . , that they may be consummated in unity," this dream of sharing God's life, a dream which might seem reserved to privileged beings or to an elite, is truly and formally realized not by an act similar to eating, but *by* eating: "I am the bread of life. I am the living bread." The life which Christ proposes to us is not only symbolized by a meal; it really is eating. Human food is a weak image for what, in the very context of nourishment, is the way God gives himself in the sacraments. Thus, two extremes meet and are joined: the most elementary and most humble activity, and the most divine act. In the end, the only things which escape devinization are the pretentious activities of the man who wants to live alone.[1]

We can say that God sanctifies our life, but we must not stop there. The sacraments offer to little ones, who are content with modest human gestures, what the Father has hidden from the wise, namely, the very secret of God and of his proper holiness. How can man accede to it? He must humbly accept to stand before God, and he must know, despite the obscurity of faith, that by such poor acts, he can "rise beyond the stars" and enter into God's mystery.

Such are the sacraments. It is not those who try to raise themselves above the human condition who will truly enter into the divine condition (reread the two banquet parables: Mt. 22:2–10 and Lk. 14:15–24, and Heb. 9).

The sacraments give something other than the fulfillment of human life, even though God respects this fulfillment. They give access to a "divine" life. They are God's response to those who doubt a supernatural life, to those who know fear in face of a life they feel is raised too high. God's response is made of the simplest gestures. "In believing my promises, you will enter into divine life, you will partake of my rest, you will share in my banquet."

God gives God to men. But God gives himself twice:

The Father gives his Son (first communication): "yes, God

loved the world so much that he gave his only Son, so that everyone who believes in him may not be lost but may have eternal life" (Jn. 3:16; cf. Jn. 6:32).

The Father and the Son give their Spirit (second communication): "I shall ask the Father, and he will give you another Advocate to be with you forever" (Jn. 14:16; cf. I Jn. 3:24).

And this is what Christ came to tell us. We are called to share in God's blessed fruitfulness; we are invited to enter into this exchange.

The great object of Christian faith is that Jesus is the *Son of God*. This is the faith which Christ expects from his disciples, and not just faith in his quality as Messiah or Savior. "We have found the Messiah," said Andrew (Jn. 1:41)—but he demands faith in the secret of his Person, a secret so divine that "neither flesh nor blood can reveal it, but only the Father who is in heaven." After he multiplied the loaves, the crowds acclaimed Jesus as the Messiah because "this really is the prophet who is to come into the world" (Jn. 6:14). But Christ *expects a higher faith*. He asks his apostles, his confidants, his witnesses: " 'But you,' he said, 'who do you say I am?' Then Simon Peter spoke up, 'You are the Christ,' he said, *'the Son of the living God' "* (Mt. 16:16). This is Christ's secret, that he is the Son of God.

To accede to this truth is to engage oneself in eternal life: "anyone who believes in the Son has eternal life" (Jn. 3:36). This is the faith which saves, and which is sealed in Baptism: "is there anything to stop me being baptized?" the Ethiopian eunuch asked the deacon Philip after he had told him the good news about Jesus. "And Philip said, 'If you believe with all your heart, you may.' And he replied, 'I believe that Jesus Christ is the Son of God' " (Acts 8:37).

This is the central point, the substance of the Apostles'

preaching: "the only knowledge I claimed to have was about Jesus, and only about him as the crucified Christ" (I Cor. 2:2). And St. Paul has just said to the Corinthians that they are called by God to be "joined to his *Son, Jesus Christ*" (I Cor. 1:9). St. Mark begins his gospel: "The beginning of the good news about Jesus Christ, the Son of God" (Mk. 1:1). And St. John: "these things are recorded so that you may believe that Jesus is the Christ, the Son of God, and that believing this you may have life through his name" (Jn. 20:31).

The good news which Jesus brings is precisely that he, the Son of God, is given to us by the Father in order to save us: "we ourselves saw and we testify that the Father sent his Son as Savior of the world" (I Jn. 4:14). And this salvation consists in *knowing the Father and the Son:* "And eternal life is this: to know you, the only true God, and Jesus Christ whom you have sent" (Jn. 17:3), and in *entering into their company:* "that life was made visible: we saw it and we are giving our testimony, telling you of the eternal life which was with the Father and has been made visible to us. What we have seen and heard we are telling you so that you too may be in union with us, as we are in union *with the Father and with his Son Jesus Christ*" (I Jn. 1:2–3). "God by calling you has joined you to his Son, Jesus Christ; and God is faithful" (I Cor. 1:9).

How is this union, this exchange with the Father and the Son, realized? By the gift they make us of their common Spirit: "we can know that we are living in him and he is living in us because he lets us share his Spirit" (I Jn. 4:13; and cf. I Jn. 3:24).

By means of the sacraments, Jesus gives his Spirit: "I have baptized you with water," said John the Baptist, "but he will baptize you with the Holy Spirit" (Mk. 1:8). The Holy

Spirit is the gift of God (Acts 8:20), which comes from the Father and the Son (Jn. 15:26). He is the Paraclete who assists the Church after Jesus' return to the Father. He unites the faithful to Jesus by remaining in them (Jn. 14:16–17). He is the Spirit of God and the Spirit of Christ; without him, we are not of Christ: "your interests are not in the unspiritual, but in the spiritual, since the Spirit of God has made his home in you. In fact, unless you possess the Spirit of Christ, you would not belong to him. . . . Everyone moved by the Spirit is a son of God" (Rom. 8:9, 14).

And so, the purpose of this "gospel," this economy of the sacraments, is to make men sons of God and adopted brothers of the unique Son:

"to all who did accept him he gave power to become *children of God*" (Jn. 1:12). "So that his Son might be the eldest of many brothers" (Rom. 8:29). "You are, all of you, sons of God through faith in Christ Jesus. All baptized in Christ, you have all clothed yourself in Christ. . . . When the appointed time came, God sent his Son, born of a woman, born a subject of the Law . . . to enable us to be adopted as sons. The proof that you are sons is that God has sent the Spirit of his Son into our hearts: the Spirit that cries, 'Abba, Father' " (Gal. 3:26 and 4:4–6).

Not only does God give God to men, but God gives himself to men as their food, in order to become simply one with them; and this is the final word of revelation.

God, in revealing himself to man's spirit, becomes his nourishment in faith, hope, and charity: he is the object of knowledge and love. In the sacraments, God becomes man's nourishment on the carnal and human level, which is inseparable from the spiritual level, in an act which will remain eternally: we eat Christ's flesh and we drink his blood.

We know the inexhaustible admiration of the Curé d'Ars in face of this mystery:

His love brought him to do what we would not have dared to ask of him. Would we have ever dared to ask God to have his Son die for us, to give us his flesh to eat and his blood to drink? If this were not true, man could have imagined things which God could not do: he would have gone further than God in the inventions of his love. This is not possible. What man cannot say and cannot conceive of, and what he would never have dared desire, God in his love has said, conceived of, and executed.

And the Curé d'Ars, in speaking of the eternal reality of the sacraments, adds: "on the day of judgment, we will see our Lord's flesh shine through the bodies of those who received him worthily on earth." It is certain that in eternity, the vital relations and exchanges which were begun on earth will attain their fullness. We know that our future life will be a perpetual exchange between the body of Christ and our resurrected body. "Anyone who eats my flesh and drinks my blood has eternal life, and I shall raise him up on the last day. . . . Anyone who eats this bread will live forever" (Jn. 6:54, 58). To be sure, the sacraments will disappear; but the reality which they enable us to receive and which they express on earth, far from disappearing, will attain such truth that signs will no longer be necessary. Christ did not present the reception of his body as a sign, but as a reality: "my body is real food." This shows us to what point God invites us to discover "things that no eye has seen and no ear has heard, things beyond the mind of man, all that God has prepared for those who love him" (I Cor. 2:9). And how does he invite us? In giving us the poorest gestures to accomplish, but also the most deeply symbolic gestures, the most "mysterious" gestures of human life, and in the first place the act of eating.[2] In the name of love, these acts will transfigure this life of terrestrial exile, as well as its dependence and separation, to unite us to God's life.

Therefore, in order to situate the sacraments, we must always start with God and with his generosity. God became flesh so that we might *incorporate* ourselves into him. It is by means of the flesh of his Son Jesus Christ that God has saved us. It is by means of faith in Christ crucified that the sinner enters the order of salvation. And we encounter our announced Savior and our proclaimed salvation in the humblest signs of life: the sacraments. When we use these signs, we publicly proclaim our faith in a living God who came to save us.

Incorporation into Christ is the completion of God's covenant with men, prepared by the Old Testament, because it is the origin and the purpose of the covenant realized by the New Testament sacraments. We can, for example, point out with what force St. Paul returns to this in his captivity epistles (cf. Eph. 2:14–22; Col. 3:14–15; also cf. Col. 2:9–10; 3:1–3; Phil. 3:10–11). Also, the author of the Epistle to the Hebrews (Heb. 9 and 3:12–14). "If in *union* with Christ we have imitated his death, we shall also imitate him in his resurrection" (Rom. 6:5).

Let us consider for a moment two key texts in St. John, which will permit us to better understand how Christ himself proposed to us the mystery of the sacraments. Chapter six in St. John's gospel gives us a map of God's intentions, before we can even speak of sacraments.[3] We should also read the two banquet parables: Lk. 14:15–24; Mt. 22:1–10. And above all, in this same perspective, we should reread the episode of the man born blind; it describes one of Christ's most typical gestures which announces the acts of the Church which are the sacraments. We must notice the different persons in this episode and how their attitudes represent those that can be seen ranged before the sacraments. The reflections that follow will be better understood if the reader has the Gospel text in front of him.

John 6:26, 32–34. These verses show us *men's expectation and Christ's purpose.* "You are not looking for me because you have seen the signs but because you have had all the bread you wanted to eat." "It is my Father who gives you the bread from heaven, the true bread which gives life to the world."—"Sir, give us that bread always."

We can note: (1) God's purpose is summarized by the idea of *gift.* In order to make it better understood, Christ opposes today's gift to the former gift which was manna. The verbs referring to Christ's gift are always in the present, because the gift is given continually and not only for a time. (2) He gives life, which manna did not (v. 49), and this gift is himself. It is the bread of God. The Jews await "something," and Christ gives *himself.* (3) And his gift goes *to all humanity.* The manna was given only to the Jews. Here Christ is speaking to the "world."

John 6:35, 48, 51. Christ's answer: "I am the bread of life."

The Jerusalem Bible mentions here that the expression "I am" (*ego eimi*) evokes the divine name revealed to Moses (Ex. 3:14; cf. Jn. 8:24); but here and in many other passages, it introduces the explanation of a parable by gesture or word. Here, Jesus is designating himself as the true bread which the manna and the bread multiplied the day before symbolized. For St. John, the expression "I am" is very precise. We might translate: I am the true bread, the authentic bread (or, the true vine, the true light).

The life which Christ proposes to us is not symbolized by eating; it *is* eating. *It is more bread than bread.* Reread verses 53 and 55. Note Christ's insistence on the word "truly." Aren't we always tempted to act as though it were only a symbolic gesture or an imaginary action which we empty of its reality?

John 6:57. Don't we often limit the sacraments to the accomplishment of a human duty or to merely putting things in moral order? Reread verse 57; it refers to the divine life and the trinitarian life itself.

Christ insists on the human realism of eating. In this text, the verb chosen by St. John signifies an astonishing realism that scandalized the Hebrews. And this sheds light on all the sacraments. Are we sufficiently attentive to the tremendous unity they realize? St. John's text insists that there is a fusion between this very simple act of eating bread and the divine act of living according to the Father. The fusion is worked by this act which is simultaneously human and divine, visible and invisible, which is called eating the flesh of Christ.

John 6:60–66. Men's answer. St. John always places on the scene persons in whom we can recognize ourselves. The reactions of these men are the reflection of our own attitudes toward the sacraments. This act is so extraordinary that many of the disciples expressed once and for all the normal and perpetual reaction of human intelligence to these words when they cried out in verse 60: "this is intolerable language. How could anyone accept it?"

Christ's answer gives us a schema for a good examination of conscience with regard to the sacraments. Let us follow this examination: v. 64, "there are some of you who do not believe"; v. 65, "this is why I told you that no one could come to me unless the Father allows him"; and at the end of the episode, v. 66, "after this, many of his disciples left him and stopped going with him."

The episode of the man born blind recapitulates, as a particular case, these same intuitions which are preliminary to every sacrament.

Are we sufficiently aware that, in the sacraments, the *initiative always comes from Christ?* Even before the blind man asks for it, Christ proposes the gift to him. Shouldn't we see in this a lesson regarding the gratuity which is the properly divine mark of every gesture of God?

Are we sufficiently conscious of the force of this prophetic act of Christ who chooses to cure a blind man in order to bring us to understand that he is the light of faith? They have eyes and they see not!

Are we disconcerted by the *modesty* of what God proposes to us? This time it is a matter of mud and saliva. God comes to meet us where we are. Wouldn't we want him to adapt his gift to our situation? If Christ chooses mud to put on the blind man's eyes as a symbol of the blindness which he has just cured, isn't this a sign that the healing seeks to adapt itself to the very infirmity of man? This is how far the Incarnation goes.

There are two elements in the blind man's attitude: (1) his confident obedience, for as he gives himself to Christ, he "goes to Siloe"; and (2) having recognized Christ, he believes in him who has cured him. *His healing led him to faith,* v. 38: "the man said, 'Lord, I believe,' and worshipped him." The blind man cooperated in God's work in two ways: by his obedience, and by his consent to another who overturned his universe.

We should examine *the attitudes of all the other participants* in this episode: the Pharisees, the parents, the Apostles.

THE SAVIOR IS PLACED IN OUR HANDS

God's works are always the result of love. And we can have no notion of their true meaning if we do not inquire into this love. What are the laws which govern God's love? How can we prevent ourselves from falling into error on this subject?

To the degree that we do not love ourselves, we already feel a certain difficulty in understanding that human love needs to do *more than is necessary* in order to manifest itself. In order to show that he truly loves, man always tries to surpass what is strictly due and to act gratuitously. We know the capital importance which everything that is gratuitous has in the order of love. In a way, the law of all love is that of "excess," because it is the law of the infinite and of gratuity.

This is still more true with regard to God. God's love is still more infinite than man's can be. And nothing that is limited, finite, or created, can fully manifest it. It needs a reality which implies transcendence.

The sacraments, like the Incarnation, witness to this transcendence and excess. We can well think that God could have saved us without the Incarnation or the sacraments, and that our salvation could have been obtained in a different way. But all of the New Testament, and especially St. John and St. Paul, make us go further and never lose sight of the divine reasons or "intentions." These are intentions of love. It is for love of us that God becomes incarnate and saves us. But, to the degree that God could have saved us without the Incarnation, it is not for love of us alone, but for him-with-us, that God sends his Son. We can go so far as to say that God wanted to have to save us, because this luxury alone permitted him to manifest the infinity of his love.[4]

So that we might not put limits to his love, God invented a way of offering us salvation. In the Incarnation and the sacraments, he does what is necessary to save us, but he also does what is more than necessary: by means of the Incarnation and the Passion, he wanted to manifest to us that his love is personal; by means of the sacraments, he wanted to make us capable of participating in the dignity of the Incarnation and capable of giving, in our turn, a personal response.

We must never forget to look at these mysteries precisely as situated in the order of an excess which cannot be explained except by love. In the final count, we must perhaps go so far as to think that if the Incarnation and the sacraments are at the center of God's salvific plan, it is for love, for this "something more," for this excess, that God has acted in this way.

Each one of us, if he is sincere, discovers this excess of love in a concrete and inevitable way from his own sinfulness. Finally, each one of us can understand this "excess" only on the day he himself has had to answer the question, "Will I have to reckon with a God of justice or a God of mercy?" It takes a lot of time to discover how God alone can really "experience the wretchedness" of another, how God alone can "be" merciful, because he alone knows and loves in an absolutely pure way. He alone can take perfect account of the other, and therefore heal his hurt while seeking nothing more than the good of the one he loves. If David cried out at the death of his son (who had nevertheless been his enemy), "My son Absalom! My son! My son Absalom! Would I had died in your place!" (II Sam. 19:1), only God could do it: he would take the place of others, he would take on everyone's hurt, and persevere to his death.

We might recall what Bergson wrote about God as Love,

particularly significant because he is a non-Christian philosopher:

.... The philosopher .... [conceives] as creative energy the love wherein the mystic sees the very essence of God.

.... Why should He need us unless it be to love us? And it is to this very conclusion that the philosopher who holds to the mystical experience must come. Creation will appear to him as God undertaking to create creators, that He may have, besides Himself, beings worthy of His love.

.... There is nothing to prevent the philosopher from following to its logical conclusion the idea which mysticism suggests to him of a universe which is the mere visible and tangible aspect of love and of the need of loving, together with all the consequences entailed by this creative emotion: I mean the appearance of living creatures in which this emotion finds its complement; of an infinity of other beings without which they could not have appeared. . . .[5]

Schillebeeckx writes:

It is as if God himself departed from his divine viewpoint and entered creation as a man in order to make this response himself to his invitation to love, by means of a perpetual living experience of the conditions of our human existence, exclusive of sin. God, the free person who invites us to love, is in his humanity at the same time the free person who accepts this love in the name of us all.[6]

Our way of regarding the sacraments as if they were only remedies or assurances or merely a help for our human development, is a scandal. We do not have the right to "practice" by putting between parentheses him who has invited us to his love and abstracting from the intentions of this practice. If God invented the sacraments, it is not only to cure us, but also to teach us the dimensions of his love.

We feel that this intuition, the law of excess, is one which can enable us to better penetrate the thought of St. Paul and St. John. There are many texts which can be cited. We can reread the two essential passages on this subject in the epistle which gives us St. Paul's theology of the cross, the Epistle to the Romans (Chapter five) and in the epistle which gives us his theology of glory, the Epistle to the Ephesians (Chapter 1).

St. John and St. Paul often speak of a "too great love" when they refer to God's attitude in our regard. When we think of God, don't we risk having our ideas distorted by the limitations inherent in our experience of human love? Aren't we too often ignorant of the gratuity and the super-abundance which are the very criteria of love?

Are we conscious of our need to examine ourselves on our utilitarian attitude toward the sacraments? Reread the episode of the disciples of Emmaus (Lk. 24:13–35): "You foolish men! So slow to believe the full message of the prophets!" Don't we sometimes merit this reproach? We are often over-eager to find a human assurance for our salvation, and we forget *why* and *by whom* we have been saved. We certainly want to benefit from salvation, because after a time we see that "we can't make it alone"; but are we convinced that with this we have not exhausted the intentions of love which God has for us?

If a mother who pulls her child out of the fire exposes herself to suffering in order to save him, she is only giving him one proof among many others of a love that is much more vast. Will he know enough to understand? And do we know enough to understand in presence of the Incarnation, the paschal mystery, and the sacraments, that by simply benefiting we are not exhausting all the motives of love present in them?

We can continue this examination of our lack of comprehension of the sacraments by asking ourselves about all the illusions we entertain concerning God's justice and mercy.

We spend a lot of time counting on the divine mercy. Is there a solution in refusing God because of evil, since precisely this refusal leaves evil without an answer? Aren't we setting ourselves off from every hope when we refuse to see evil in the light of God? When we ally our cause with God's, don't the sacraments help us to admit that entering a little more into the mystery of evil is to enter a little more into the mystery of God, and vice versa?

Are we willing to recognize that God in his mercy is inimitable? The divine mercy has no common measure with our experience of human mercy. We try to alleviate misery, but isn't it most of the time because of compassion or justice rather than mercy? Because we find the sight of evil unbearable, the desire to heal it arises in us from our need to soften the pain we feel. When compassion is sufficiently alive in us to provoke us to act, isn't it rather to free our conscience than for love of the other that we act? Or, having received more than the person who is suffering, don't we act because of a desire to repair the damage, in the name of justice alone?

In face of our sin, do we dare to *choose* God's mercy? Answering a Sister who was defending the rights of divine justice, St. Thérèse de Lisieux declared, "Sister, you want justice from God, you will get justice from God. The soul receives exactly what it expects from God." And, "I expect as much from the good God's justice as from his mercy; it is because he is just that he is compassionate and filled with mildness, slow to punish and abounding in mercy."[7]

What then is this transcendence, this "excess," which the
sacraments offer us? It goes much farther than we might think.
We know that God saves us, that he wanted to make us not
only heirs of salvation but also "cooperators" in this salvation (I Cor. 3:9). And there is still more in the sacraments:
God establishes us in the dignity of the Son of God himself.
Not only does God call us servants of salvation, but his
"sons."

The sacraments give us a new way of sharing in the life of
God. In the final count, is there anything greater or more
mysterious in the situation of the priest, the baptized, or the
confirmed? Over and above any activity, they are bound to
Christ the Savior and participate in his task, grace, and function. And, by this gift, every Christian is in a way present to
the mystery which makes the man Jesus the Son of God in
person. Thus, every Christian is reclothed with a sacerdotal
dignity which is greater than the sacraments themselves, the
Eucharist or the remission of sins, and on which depend all
the sacraments. The human creature participates in the grace
by which Christ was able to institute the sacraments. It is
more essential for a branch to be grafted to the vine than to
bear fruit. The sacraments simultaneously give sap and fruit,
by means of a superabundant richness which cannot be exhausted in a single expression. They give us grace and at the
same time they dispose us to receive it.

By means of the sacraments, God makes us "surplus humanities" for his Son; by means of them we extend in time
and space the very acts which Christ posited during his human life. For example, the Mass is not only the renewal of
the cross and Resurrection, which were two separate acts; it is
the very act of Christ the Savior, existing at this moment in
this place. And the same is true for every sacrament: God
wanted men to have the powers of his Son at their disposal,

in such a way that this dignity cannot be lost, even if we want to break with him. The baptized, the confirmed, the priest, remain what they are for eternity, even if they want to separate themselves from God.

In this, there is a new identification between man and God. It implies an infinite dignity for man, anterior to every work of salvation, more sublime than the cross and resurrection themselves, namely, that Jesus is God, and that by means of the sacraments we are invited to the same dignity. The cross and the resurrection are splendid fruits of this divine dignity, but they remain inferior to it. "If you are the body of Christ, it is your own mystery that you receive. To what you are, you answer 'Amen,' and your answer is a commitment. You hear pronounced, 'The body of Christ,' and you answer, 'Amen'" (St. Augustine).

God has wanted this in virtue of the gratuitous superabundance which presided over the Incarnation. And this is certainly a real transcendence. The coming of the Son of God in the Incarnation realizes the union with God which, though it is subordinate to salvation, surpasses the simple fact of being saved. The same light can enable us to measure the mystery of the sacraments and that of the Incarnation. In fact, the sacraments are nothing but the acts of Christ the Savior continued by the body of the faithful, the Church, in time and space. "Blessed fault" (*felix culpa*), because it brings us much farther than we might have thought. Blessed liberty, which, even in its failings, obliges us to discover the grandeur of our destiny and how far salvation goes.

Are we convinced of the originality of the salvation which Christ gives us? In what does this originality consist? Do we give proper consideration not only to the absolute gratuity of God's gift, but to his *expectation in our regard?* Granted "we are fellow-workers with God," as St. Paul says (I Cor. 3:9); do we take "fellow-workers" and "cooperators" seriously? Pius XII said that "Christ needs the help of his members." Is this a reality for us? (Reread Col. 1:24.) This truth was already present in God's call in the Old Testament (cf. Ex. 19:5–6; Jer. 2:3; Is. 61:6; Deut. 7:6). St. Peter uses very expressive words to refer to this dignity which is our priesthood: "chosen race, royal priesthood." (Reread I Pet. 2:9; Rev. 1: 5–6; Jn. 17:18–19.)

Do we give their full force to *the relationships between Christ and ourselves, in the practice of the sacraments?* St. Paul speaks most forcefully of our unity with Christ; he almost creates his own words for what he is trying to express (cf. Eph. 2:5): God "brought-us-to-life-with" Christ, "raised-us-up-with" him, and "gave-us-a-place-with" him; we are "created-in" Christ Jesus.

At Mass, are we conscious of the fact that it does not only represent the Last Supper, calvary, and the Resurrection for us, but that we are participating with Christ in the very act of salvation? We are assimilated, incorporated, to such a point in Christ Jesus that we live the saving act itself. We might reread the preface, the prayer after the consecration, and the conclusion of the canon of the Mass, as well as the expressive texts in which St. Paul describes our incorporation into Christ, the foundation of the whole gospel teaching on the sacraments (Eph. 2:15–22; Gal. 3:27–29).

We find ourselves under a continual difficulty in our relationships with God. We stand before Someone who surpasses us, and we must enter a plan which is not ours. So, in a way, the sacraments completely modify our relationships with God. The consequence of the new dignity to which the sacraments elevate us is that we are obliged to go still farther in comprehending God's love.

We make of God's body exactly what we want. We use it or we do not. We abuse it or we adore it, without God being able to do anything about it, because he put himself in our hands once and for all as a man. Through his Son, God is the author of our salvation. He wanted to be handed over to us under this aspect also. The horrors of war have taught us to what point men can be handed over to other men: Auschwitz, Ravensbrück, and Dachau. After Calvary, these names can remind us of the degree to which God himself wanted to be handed over into our power. "This is my body given over for the forgiveness of many." Christ *really* gave himself and handed himself over to us.

By means of the sacraments, we are masters of our Savior. Thus, to a degree, in the order of terrestrial things according to which God has intended our salvation, everything depends on our good pleasure. We see Christ's body put into the hands of men, and therefore *salvation is put into their hands, a thing which, on this plane, totally reverses our relationship of dependence on God.* There results an accentuation of the *initiative left to the believer* in the work of salvation, in virtue of which God comes *to reconcile infinite respect for our liberty with the evident truth which he gives to everything and which the creature can only receive.* In affirming that God places salvation in our hands, we say that he respects our liberty, and we like to repeat it to ourselves. We naturally like to think that whatever the roads intended by God, he will not save us without us. His work supposes, as a minimum, this simple consent on our part: that we not put an obstacle in the way. *But God wants to go much farther than this when he respects our liberty and proposes that we ourselves cooperate in our salvation.*

To be sure, only God and Christ are and remain the source

of our supernatural life. But in using the sacraments in faith, we participate gratuitously in this power to be ourselves the source of this life in us and to be masters of the acts which decide our personal salvation. In faith renewed by the sacraments, our liberty extends its power not only to the exercise of the supernatural life, but to the very source of this life which nevertheless comes only from God. It is as though man fully becomes the creator of his own destiny. This is the astonishing return proposed to us and accomplished by the sacraments: we have God at our disposition at the very moment when we renounce our disposition of ourselves and of him, when we place ourselves entirely at the disposition of his grace which is present in each sacrament.

In conferring Baptism, man raises up a new creature, a new child of God; he participates in the creative power of the Word. In asking for Baptism and in receiving it freely, man has an efficacious hold on the creative power of God, exactly in the same way as he is efficacious in face of the daily realities of his existence.

It is with an infinite delicacy that God does everything he can to depend on man in the work of salvation, in so far as he can without ceasing to be God. And this goes much farther (but in another direction) than what every man sometimes dreams of: to be his own master. Sin is nothing else than this dream of independence pushed to the absolute. In his own way God answers our dream of finding a domain of activities which finally depends only on ourselves. In this we should read God's will to respect us as "persons" resembling him and to bestow on us this dignity of being master of our life and our destiny. In this way, in the sacraments, God lays salvation in our hands, as he would hand us a child.

We can say that in the sacraments the priest is God's in-

strument and that this means that it is God and not the priest
who realizes the eucharistic mystery. The priest is the instrument of this mystery in as humble a way as a pen is the instrument of the person who is writing. But to be God's
instrument in this way, he must decide to do so; it is only in
this sense—which goes terribly far—that he is an intelligent
instrument of the divine action. And it is equally in this
sense that all Christians are intelligent instruments of their
salvation; they themselves unleash the infinite power of the
supernatural order when and as they want it. And they have
the same power to abuse it.

The Incarnation goes so far as to put the Son of God at the
disposition of men. God places Christ's body in their hands so
that they can do with it exactly what they want, but he asks
them to use it for their salvation. In virtue of the Incarnation, God reverses the relationship between him and the creature: inasmuch as he is God, he dominates everything and
the creature depends. This truth can in no way disappear.
But inasmuch as he is man, it is he who depends on the creature. He gives himself to the creature, in a total passivity.
which is an image of the passivity he asks of the creature in
his regard: "You see how I hand myself over to you; profit
from it; it is in order to teach you to place yourself in turn
in my hands." It is so difficult for the rebellious creature to
accept his incredible poverty that, in order to encourage
him, God has placed himself in an analogous poverty.

WE COME TO BE CURED AND PROGRESS

"Here I am at the end of my journey; I am in prison!" I repeated
to myself every minute. "I am in port for long, very long years.

This is my corner! I arrive here with my heart pounding, full of apprehension and defiance. . . . But who knows if, when the time comes to leave it many years from now, I may regret it!" The thought that I would one day regret leaving this place filled me with an agonizing horror.

Do we know to what degree we are imprisoned? And do we really want to leave our prisons? "When it comes time, will I regret leaving this place?" Dostoyevsky asked, and it was indeed of the prisons that he was speaking in his *Memories of the House of the Dead.*

We have seen that the purpose of the sacraments is to assimilate us to God's life and to make us masters of our destiny by making us the source of our liberty and salvation. They have still another purpose: to cure us and to draw us step by step, according to the events of our life, out of our sickness and immaturity. Thus, the sacraments suggest to us that we come out of the prison in which we are kept by our illusions, habits, and the weight of our faults. But they can do this only on one condition, namely, by revealing to us how much our life is dominated by the law of sin and the law of progress.

The lives of the saints have taught us what courage must support this lucidity and what illusions each one of us must escape. We remember St. Thérèse de Lisieux's answer to her sister who said to her, "when I look at you I feel discouraged, because I think of how much I still have to acquire!" "Oh, no, no, do not say 'to acquire,' but 'to lose.' "

The Curé d'Ars gave a similar answer to a lady who came to see him, and who was very happy to finally have the chance to meet him: "Oh, Father," she said, "how good it is to finally see you. I know myself so little, I so need, so want to know myself; and everyone has said how clairvoyant you are. . . ."

And the Curé d'Ars answered, "Madam, you are very fortu-
nate to know yourself so little; if you knew only half, you
would no longer be able to stand yourself."

In calling us to share his friendship, God is not calling us to
illusion. Any life with God can be born and exist only in desire for light, because it is a life founded on love. Therefore,
when we enter into friendship with God, we must accept that
he seriously means to form our well-being and to draw us out
of the illusion that menaces us at every instant. If Christ, the
Son of God, began his life with a fight for truth against the
temptations in the desert, and ended it with the battle which
was his agony, how can it be otherwise for us?

What can a doctor do for someone who does not want to
know that he is sick? What can a savior do for someone who
does not want to come out of his prison? In his encounters
with men, Jesus never seeks to dissimulate their weakness,
sin, or sickness. God's first way of manifesting himself in a life
is to bestow the gift of lucidity. Christ cannot come without
revealing what is, simply what is, like a light that adds
nothing but enables us to see reality. Christ hid nothing of
what they were from the Samaritan woman, from St. Peter,
from Mary Magdalen, from Matthew, from the publican:
weak beings and sinners. And how happy he is when the
centurion or Zachaeus accepts the light! But what deception
he feels in face of the Pharisees!

Christ is received only by those who have recognized their
inability to organize their existence by themselves, that is,
those who have admitted that their life is dominated by the
law of sin and the law of progress. We are not merely adolescents who need to learn how to become men; we are also invalids wounded by sin and consequently incapable not only
of finding salvation or attaining the fullness of adult age with-

out a long delay, but even of using the means for our cure.

It is quite natural to be afraid of discovering one's cancer and not to be eager to leave one's prison, if it means that we must then worry about our existence alone. It is normal not to want to be reconciled to the miserable character of the human condition at this price. To be alone in face of one's distress is too hard. It is not enough to give us remedies if we do not know how to use them. This is why the sacraments are not simple medicines, but *the presence of Someone* who begins by showing us how we need to be healed. It is not enough to give us the germ of a divine life which we will have to encourage along more or less quickly; we need to be cured of a mortal sickness which prevents us from correctly using this source of supernatural life and almost infallibly impels us to let it languish. "And if your heart condemns you, God is greater than your heart" (I Jn. 3:20).

God has multiplied the sacraments around the Eucharist in face of this situation, in order to answer the many needs of a sick person. We might ask why there are so many sacraments. We can look for some direction or order in them. But it is at the moment that we discover the encounter between God's mercy and the concrete conditions of man's life, that we most surely understand the secret of the economy which the sacraments realize. Then they appear to us *admirably adapted for the prudent convalescence* which we need to enter progressively into God's Kingdom.

Each sacrament is therefore an expedient of the divine pedagogy, adapted not only to human nature, but to its wounded and growing *condition*. In order to offer us a share in his life, God takes account of the fact that we complete ourselves in time, by means of gifts and setbacks. And God places himself in the forefront of all the great experiences we have as men; and he does this by means of the sacraments. He takes them to his account. There is not any experience that cannot be governed by a gesture of Christ, including failures and the battle against death. For man who is on the way, every sacrament is "viaticum." By means of it, we progressively, slowly, and daily realize Christ's life.

Let us therefore meditate a bit on each sacrament and, without indulging in cheap concordances, let us simply inquire what great human experiences are found behind each one of them. We are not trying to prove that it is not stupid that there are seven sacraments; rather, we want to do much more: we want to discover to what depths God comes to help us to live the great experiences which are ours day after day, and especially the moments when, like the disciples on the road to Emmaus, we no longer really believe in the seriousness of our own existence. It is true that sometimes the sacraments educate our life in spite of us; there are days when we know better how far God goes to save this life which doesn't seem to matter much anymore.

And so there is a sacrament for the beginning: Baptism; a sacrament for maturity: Confirmation; a sacrament for the successive times we have to get up again and which progressively purifies us: Penance; a sacrament to heal the body of its suffering and for the fight against death: Anointing of the Sick. And there are the sacraments of adult age and the communication of life: Matrimony which takes care of the gift of self and the human fruitfulness of love, and Orders which consecrates to the spiritual common good those whom God has chosen to be the servants of his people.

Finally, there is the sacrament which administers to us, drop by drop and mercifully, the dose of eternal nourishment which can support us until we have attained our measure; at that moment, the Eucharist will disappear as a sacrament to appear as an eternal reality.

We are not only children, but also invalids. And God has borrowed the signs he uses, sometimes from the normal development of a healthy life (food, marriage, confirmation), sometimes from acts that repair our deficiencies and from daily tasks which enable us to fight against sickness. "When death was what they deserved, you have given them time and room to rid themselves of wickedness" (Wis. 12:20).

We should learn from the sacraments the seriousness of our human experiences. God never contradicts this. We see Christ in the gospel preparing very carefully to institute the sacraments as he bends to the situations of men. Christ's mercy comes to help us so that we may not have to live our experiences alone.

It is difficult and even impossible for a man to fulfill everything that belongs to his task as a father; God associates himself with this task by means of Baptism. It is hard to have the courage to meet evil and fight against it. It is hard to accept responsibility for others. It is still harder to remain faithful during one's entire existence to a human love. And who can pretend not to be afraid of suffering and death? Who would dare to say that he has never feared being alone in the course of his existence or that he has never feared being alone in the future, if our good God had not given himself to us to be present with us day after day and to reassemble all men around his Eucharist and the sacraments?

The gospel shows that Christ prepared the sacraments according to and corresponding to different events in the life of men. Are we sufficiently attentive to how close Christ is to us in the different circumstances of our life because of this? Reread, for example, for *Baptism,* the episode of Nicodemus

(Jn. 3:1–21) and the episode of the man born blind (Jn. 9). For *Confirmation:* Mt. 10:6–16; Jn. 7:37–39; Jn. 4:35–38. For *Penance:* Lk. 7:36–50; 23:28–43. For the *Eucharist:* Jn. 6:26–70; 12:2. For *Matrimony:* Jn. 2:1–11. For the *Anointing of the Sick:* Mt. 8:8; 9:35; Lk. 10:8. For *Orders:* Jn. 4:35–38; Lk. 10:1–20.

Are we convinced that to neglect the sacraments is not realistic? Are we convinced, concretely, that the act by which we come to possess God is not merely "spiritual"? A man's primary honesty must consist in recognizing that his is the condition of a sinner and in admitting that before God, as in every love, he is in the obscurity of faith in which he can know only "in part" (I Cor. 13:12). The sacraments adapt the eternal reality to this terrestrial condition; and the eternal reality is not purely spiritual, because it is man in his entirety who is meant to enter into the possession of God.

NOTES

1. *The consequences of the Incarnation.* In his presentation of the sacraments according to St. John, W. K. Grossouw summarizes C. H. Dodd, *The Interpretation of the Fourth Gospel,* Cambridge, 1953. In his book, *Spirituality of the New Testament* (New York: Herder & Herder, 1961), pp. 171–172, Professor W. K. Grossouw writes: "Here we face what is indeed a paradox: the most spiritual and unworldly Gospel presses the whole material creation into its service. Matter is not only accepted; it is elevated and illumined with a divine light. John draws all his conclusions from the incarnation of our Lord, which he dramatically terms 'becoming flesh.' . . . This compelled every well-intentioned reader to make his decision right from the very first page.

"That all things came into being through the Logos, that in Him was light and life, and that darkness stood in opposition to Him; with all this a person could cope, and it might even appear vaguely familiar to the Hellenist. But that the divine Word had become flesh was as great a scandal to this type of reader, as was to the Jew the notion that this man should be God. This sort of situation is frequent in John. If in the first portion of the discourse between Jesus and Nicodemus (3:1–13) we were to omit a single word, it would almost seem that we were dealing with a philosophical dialogue on the supremacy of the spirit to matter and the necessity of a purely spiritual rebirth for every man. But that one word 'water' (v. 5) is the tenuous yet firm thread which unites the whole episode with the Christian economy of matter sanctified by the Spirit of God. In 6:63 we read: 'It is the spirit that gives life; the flesh profits nothing.' Here you might think that the evangelist is again deprecating the material. But we must remember that he, no less than Paul, is fond of expressing his thoughts in antitheses. He wants to say that matter, when not viewed in relationship to Christ and informed by His Spirit, is dead and useless.

"The whole material world points to Christ as its proper meaning and fulfillment."

"Christ left us nothing purely material, but in material realities everything is spiritual. The same is true for Baptism: by means of a material gesture, the water is given to us; what is accomplished is spiritual—it is a birth and renewal. If you were without a body, Christ would have given you purely spiritual gifts; but because your soul is intimately bound to your body, he transmits spiritual goods in material realities" (St. John Chrysostom).

2. "*A sacred meal,* by itself and without the need of anything else, actually constitutes the richest hierophany there is. It is in the sacred meal that man sees the sacredness of life, of his own life, and as a result apprehends himself as being dependent upon one who is almighty and all good, or, to express it more accurately, upon the singular and superabundant fruitfulness of the divinity. To recognize the sacredness of a meal as being the highest form of human activity is to recognize man's total dependence, both for his creation and for his continued existence, upon a God who is at the same time apprehended as the one who possesses the fullness of life." (L. Bouyer: *Rite and Man,* Indiana: University of Notre Dame Press, 1963), p. 84. Cf. G. Van der Leeuw, *La religion dans son essence et ses manifestations,* pp.

339–340, and Robertson Smith, *Religion of the Semites,* London, 1927, who was the first to clarify the fundamental identity between the primitive sacred meal and sacrifice.

3. For the exegesis of this passage, and the arguments and agreements regarding its sacramental bearing, cf. A. Feuillet, *Etudes johanniques,* Desclée de Brouwer, 1962, ch. 3: "Les thèmes bibliques majeurs du discours sur le Pain de vie" (with a detailed bibliography), pp. 47–129 (reprinted in the collection "Foi vivante," Paris, 1967, *Le discours sur le Pain de vie*). English trans: *Johannine Studies* (Staten Island, N.Y.: Alba House, 1965).

4. *"God has willed to save us":* We are touching here on a very serious point of the Christian mystery which should not be reserved to a circle of initiates or theologians, because it puts into question our very reason for existing: Can we say that God wanted to have to save us?

At first sight we might easily enough be scandalized by the thought that God might have wanted to have to save us, creating man with one hand, and with the other "laying a trap in which he would be sure to fall, in order to have the pleasure of pulling him out of it."

When we are discussing God, we always risk attributing to Him an inadequate and gross human psychology. But this is no reason to abstain from saying anything. We say that God created for His glory and for love; and these two are expressions which, if we twist them, can fall prey to caricature: for example, God creating for us to admire him! and enjoying the smell of incense; or God creating because He needs us and because He gets bored with solitude. If the Church's tradition has nevertheless kept these expressions, it is because they have another deeper and more difficult sense which we must have the courage to reach.

The same is true for the affirmation which we feel we should maintain, namely, that "He wanted to have to save us." Having decided to respect the liberty of His creatures (and it is a great mystery, but the contrary would be unworthy of God), He could not "be ignorant" (this would be still more unworthy of God) of what would actually result from the wrong use of this liberty. Since the time of Christ, the Church's reflection has exhausted itself in trying to reconcile this infallible foresight with respect for a perfectly real liberty. And all during this same time, the Church has affirmed both and sustained with St. Augustine that God would never have permitted the evil had He not been able to draw a greater good out of it. Therefore, He wanted to permit the evil, because He saw that in offering salvation to us, He offered us *more* than sin caused us to lose. Therefore, He did want to have to save us, without there being any other trap than the fact of liberty itself. If we do not make a caricature out of this way of looking at things by a rather heavy anthropomorphism, we might find it difficult, it might startle us, but we will not reduce it to "nonsense," because it obliges us to admit that salvation will always be greater than the ideas we can conceive of it. Cf. M.-D. Molinié, *Le combat de Jacob* (Paris: Ed. du Cerf, 1966).

5. Henri Bergson, *The Two Sources of Morality and Religion*, trans. by R. Ashley Audra and Cloudesley Brereton (New York: Henry Holt and Co., 1935), pp. 243–244. Reprinted with the permission of Holt, Rinehart and Winston, Inc.

6. E. Schillebeeckx, *Mary, Mother of the Redemption* (New York: Sheed & Ward, 1964), p. 96.

7. St. Thérèse de Lisieux, *Manuscrits autobiographiques*, éd. 1955, vol. II, p. 61, and "Lettre au P. Roulland," May 9, 1897.

6 Sacraments and Symbols

What do the sacraments profess to be? Everything flows from God's desire to adapt his life to the life of man. This implies a twofold truth: the sacraments are simultaneously symbols, which conform to human nature, and causes, which conform to the divine action which is always efficacious. It is precisely this twofold character which makes the sacraments mysteries. The fact that these two aspects are inseparable is not evident. One always has the tendency to blur the other one out of our minds. There is no question of reducing them to a unity, but we must see each one of them in its mysterious force.

The sacraments are symbols and signs of God. They are symbols, and what symbols! When we watch a ceremony, whether it be the Mass or one of the sacraments and its signs (water, anointing, etc.), we find recapitulated all the poetry that any religion or any psychological experience might dream of. God is master of things as he is of words. The sacraments reveal to us a divine pedagogy which gives us the hundredfold through the language of things.

The sacraments are causes of our divine life. We must not be satisfied to stop at this symbolic richness; we must go further and see the sacraments in all of their force as causes. We must understand that even without this symbolical richness they would still be efficacious instruments of God's gift. The Mass celebrated in a few words in a concentration camp,

far from any spoken symbol, is as efficacious as all other ceremonies. The extraordinary richness of the sacraments in what
they have essentially, which is their sharing in God's life, can
accommodate itself to an extreme poverty of signs.

This is the paradox: richness and poverty. We must not
confuse the two orders, or we run the risk of emptying out
the mystery. It is not merely because they are rich in symbols
that the sacraments give us grace, but because they are instruments and acts of God. Certainly, the sign gives grace; but as
marvelous as the pedagogy of this symbol may be for faith,
what it gives is still richer.

What sacrament is more paradoxical than Matrimony? A
consent, an answer, decide everything forever. Everything is
finished, everything is bound. And yet, nothing has been
realized; everything remains to be constructed day after day.
This shows us to what point the sacraments grasp our existence. As in Matrimony, each step is decisive; and yet
everything remains to be done. The Eucharist gives us the
body of God, but we must be faithful until the time of eternal life. Penance gives us forgiveness, but then we have to
combat to the "point of death."[1] Baptism makes us a child of
God, but our true appearance remains to be born. Everything is acquired; nothing has been won. As in marriage, we
have the course of an adventure to run.

This paradox is at the very center of St. Paul's thought. In
two passages of the Epistle to the Romans (6:1-4; 8:1-18) in
which he describes Christian life as nourished by the sacraments, we find him insisting on the same thing. It is a state
which seems definitive, because it is pictured as a death, but
it should unceasingly be conquered or consolidated or ex-
ploited. Grace is given by right, but it becomes a real possession only by continued effort. It is a gift of grace, because

"when we were baptized we went into the tomb with him and joined him in death, so that as Christ was raised from the dead by the Father's glory, we too might live a new life" (Rom. 6:4). There is a question of voluntarily realizing what we should consider to be the result acquired by Baptism: "you should offer yourselves to God, and consider yourselves dead men brought back to life" (6:13), "Consider yourselves to be dead to sin but alive for God in Christ Jesus."

In the same way, we are "under grace," because "our former selves have been crucified with him to destroy this sinful body and to free us from the slavery of sin" (6:6). But effort is necessary: "you must not let sin reign in your mortal bodies or command your obedience to bodily passions" (6:12), "if you agree to serve and obey a master you become his slave. You cannot be slaves of sin that leads to death and at the same time slaves of obedience that leads to righteousness" (6:16). And further, "though your body may be dead it is because of sin, but if Christ is in you then your spirit is life itself because you have been justified" (8:10). However, "if by the Spirit you put an end to the misdeeds of the body you will live" (8:13).

These texts show us the same paradox: what we suppose we have acquired by Baptism—in the fact of becoming Christian —must continually be reconquered and realized at every instant by an effort that can fail. The sacrament gives only the first fruits, pledges or a deposit for our salvation. The Christian life consists in transforming this hope and possibility into reality and this partial possession into a total possession. But the important thing is that in this quest we are not alone.

God lived this human adventure before us in acts which can become ours. Christ took bread and wine to unite his

friends; he fought against suffering and evil; he loved his
Father and thanked him; he laid his hands upon the sick;
he sat at table at a marriage celebration; he saw and hated
sin and treason; he feared death; and finally, he loved humanity, the Church, as we love a woman. In this way, Christ
consecrated the acts of human life in taking them up. He
blessed our dialogue with things.

From then on, when we take bread and wine to bring men
together, when we fight against sin even to the cross, when
two persons choose each other because they love each other,
the adventure can no longer be banal; it has become holy.
From then on the life of man unites a human adventure and
a divine history. The acts and paradoxes of our life have become those of the Incarnation itself, and they take on a sense
which surpasses and completes them. Christ denies nothing
of the life of man or of this incredible creative power which
each one of us has with regard to his own life.

Our life is not all prefabricated; we really have the power
to transform its conditions. For this, we live in a state of
dialogue with things and beings; we fight to give events their
true meaning. This combat with realities is necessary for us
to construct our existence day after day and to give it its full
expansion.[2] We have to make the humblest realities work
for us—water, light, bread and wine; the supper table, sign of
friendship, and the hand, sign of contract. From then on, all
our acts can fully become sym-bols; this is to say, according
to the etymological sense, they have the power of holding-
together not only the spirit and things, but also the spirit
and God.

But although Christ denied nothing of man's life, we ourselves often lose its meaning. What has been said about
poetry is valid for our entire life: "although it manifests

itself everywhere, poetry occurs for only a few." For us, this concerns primarily a true sense for the realities which construct a life. We live on the surface of ourselves "and do not enter in except to die," as Bernanos has said.

We are often tempted by a kind of "adultery" with realities. We use them without respecting their consistency, laws, and development; we use them as greedily and gluttonously as books and magazines and television use the sexual life. It is difficult not to try to merely profit from things, whether we produce them or enjoy them, desire them or possess them. We can never sufficiently guard against this "inflation" which runs the risk of perverting everything.[3] It takes a lot of strength not to live merely on impressions and not to remain only on the surface of images and not to be a mere tourist in one's own existence.[4]

However it may appear, there is another attitude which is neither more noble nor deeper. We can be tempted to lean back on the mere power of reasoning. It is very attractive to think that we hold events, beings, or things in our possession, because we have measured them and submitted them to the calculations of reasoning. It is true that the dimensions of the universe are changing and that we must banish sentimentality. It is true that we should use all the instruments of analysis and means for knowledge which contemporary research offers us. And we are proud of them . . . like the professor who brought his five year old son to a psychiatrist to purge him beforehand of every image, symbol, or sentiment, so that only reason would govern his life, or like priests who ask if there is any sense in speaking about God's love, since love necessarily has affective aspects!

Pierre Emmanuel has said that "to analyse a symbol intellectually is to peel an onion in order to find the onion."

The effort which some people make to express all of our life in clear formulas is useless. There is nothing which can dry up a spirit so radically as to pretentiously isolate the rational. If we demythologize everything, what will remain of our life?

Things have a meaning; life demands to be discovered. Neither the need to be excited nor intellectual dryness are signs of depth, even if they imitate depth. Can the man who does not learn to listen to things and to open himself to them, pretend to be living in reality? Why man and woman? Why friendship and suffering? Why the hand and the face? Why time and expectation? Why death?

When we turn away from these questions, we make ourselves incapable of understanding the sacraments. We cannot anesthetize reality. If we ignore them, if we do not go beyond them, the symbols which are everywhere in our lives take their revenge, in a terrible way.

CAN WE DO WITHOUT SYMBOLS?

Who can avoid the attraction of the unusual? Although we can admit readily enough that not everything can be expressed by clear ideas, we find that we want to demythologize and dissociate from the affective and the religious everything which is not clear. But the only way of understanding symbols and of avoiding their cunning attacks and neutralizing their unhealthy effects, is to incorporate them into a movement which surpasses us.

We cannot do without this reflection, because the sacraments act in the way of symbols when they bring us the divine life, and their effectiveness is always in the line of what they signify.

At times, we are tempted to believe that the life of the

spirit can be exercised by disengaging ourself from all sensibility in a "pure" state. This is never true. Even abstract words cover over images, experiences, and memories that are heavy with concrete paste, heavy with sensible reality. For example, the word "fatherland" immediately brings to mind the image of our flag, the Fourth of July, readings and drawings that we knew in childhood, paratroopers, or military cemeteries, etc. Each word rests on several layers (think of such words as liberty, sin, etc.). Every "word" holds together an idea and an experience; the symbol is that which "holds-with."[5] As soon as a reality of the mind is not alone, we can say that it has the force of symbol. The bread and wine are no longer alone: they are "with" Christ; and the same is true of everything which exists in our daily life.

For each one of us, some things are more charged with significance than others; they excite desire or aggressiveness more than others. Each one of us possesses a personal mental universe and bathes in an atmosphere which holds him entirely, as absolutely as a philosophy and the power of a magical charm.

The role of these image-forces is an *affective role* which acts like a spell. From this arises the kind of suspicion in which serious minds are tempted to enclose everything that has to do with symbols, and which therefore influences their thoughts on the sacraments. We are often tempted to relegate them to the domain of the morbid or of an artistic pastime.

We try to empty out mythologies; and we see them come right back stronger. We remain dominated by archetypes and myths which are all the more fearsome in that they are unconscious. We certainly must surpass mythology, but we cannot rid ourselves of it by our own strength alone any more than we can make tuberculosis disappear by means of a simple x-ray.

The symbol answers a need in human nature much more profound than the artistic need. And its serious use corresponds to quite another thing than a sickness. It is dangerous to try to purge ourselves of symbols too quickly and to believe that our thought liberated in this way will suffice to purify the obscure forces of the imagination. Let us consider a few examples.

We always attribute magic to primitive peoples, and not to adult and evolved civilizations.[6] However, from the Nüremberg stadium where the cult of a Führer was celebrated, to the clubs which are always forming around the stars of stage and screen, how many men have succumbed to the magical hypnotism of the photo of their idols or the swastika! The serious gentlemen at Rotary Club dinners and the Legion of Mary meetings are as eager to use secret signs as are the Boy Scouts. And this is not merely a question of fantasy or amusement for adolescents of every age. One of reason's most foolish illusions is to think that it is sheltered from being contaminated with things.

It takes the violence of death to show us the symbolic place which some things have in our life; and it is in this way that the death of President Kennedy was felt by many as a personal mourning. And we felt something as strong, perhaps stronger, at the time when Pope John XXIII died. Protestants felt themselves brothers with Catholics for having all lost a father; all of humanity had become used to this Pope's face as the image of paternal goodness.

Other events show us every day the spell which symbols exercise. The disappearance of certain persons and the loss we feel at their absence, enables us to measure the place which they occupied in the lives of millions of men. And it unarms those who would like to explain everything in refusing mystery its part. The reactions of even the most rationalistic persons after the suicide of a star like Marilyn Monroe furnished a striking example.[7]

Man finds it hard to accept being a religious animal, and yet he never stops reinventing his gods.[8] No matter how much we try to block them out, how many events, bearers of infinitely more than themselves, raise up before our eyes symbols and nourishment for the life of the spirit? Each one of these examples shows us that it is not in refusing symbols that man can be cured of magical groupings, but by going *right to the end* of the religious need he feels in events that bear the symbol. Beyond Marilyn Monroe's telephone call as she was about to commit suicide, he must see the terrifying solitude of a happiness made to man's measure; beyond Kennedy's death, the force of a sacrifice for the common good; beyond the face of John XXIII, paternity; beyond Paul VI's voyage to Palestine, faith in the love which can unite men.

Neither did Christ refuse symbols; he lived them and chose them with love. In instituting the great prophetic acts of humanity, he permitted us to no longer fear the excess of our sensibility, because he showed us the way to surpass it. But there have always been Pharisees to think that the confusion of Mary Magdalene or of the Samaritan woman, the popular enthusiasm of Palm Sunday, or the call of the Good Thief had nothing to do with something religious.

It is quite legitimate to want to cure man and to give him a larger dominion over himself by making him explore the hidden zones of his conscience or of his past. It is not surprising that we discover that those among us, sick or not, who thought themselves freed of their imagination, find emotion-

ally charged symbols in their "affective" life under the unconscious domination of events and great image-types.

Without reducing psychoanalysis to the explanation of
man by his sexual life, the history of these last years is a significant example of the symbol's revenge on the life of men.[9]
It is wrong to think that, in the name of falsely religious or
socially forbidden motives, we are rid of one of the most
violent forces of human nature (the one which prolongs its
existence) by merely wanting to ignore it, to refuse it, or to
damn it.

We must recognize the harmful influence that Puritanism
and Jansenism had. But we should also recognize that they
are quite external accidents of Anglo-Saxon Protestantism or
French civilization. When we examine the Bible or writings
previous to the seventeenth century in France, we find that
they treat of sexual things with a simplicity that is sometimes
respectful and sometimes jolly, but which shows that these
men thought of sexual life as it is, with its image value for
the profound meaning of human life.

Under the pretext of freeing man from his carnal condition, we suppress the profound character of this condition to
make it into something as material as the act of drinking a
glass of water. The result is simple: instead of being freed,
man falls sick from it. The revenge is amazing; and it is
proof that we do not exorcise sexuality so easily, because it
"holds-with" it something more than itself and it impreg-
nates our whole way of being.

The psychoanalysts' itinerary—especially Freud's—is significant. In the beginning they thought that they could rationally
demythologize every sexual taboo. They were later obliged
to give citizenship to the imaginary and to recognize its positive force. And in bringing the symbolism of sexual life to

light, they discovered that it cannot be balanced or cured by its own forces alone, or by the force of reason alone, but that it is necessary to use something which surpasses it. They had to recognize that in the most primitive forces of man, of which sexuality is only one aspect, there is a call to something else. Neither do psychologists seek merely to rationalize sexuality or to de-symbolize what is symbolic in it, but rather, they are careful to point out the call to surpass it which works the reconciliation of man's different forces and which unifies his desire.

Why is the carnal life with its relationships of filiation and paternity so serious, if not because it is the symbol of our attitudes toward Another? Acceptance of our own limitations, solitude, dependence, or refusal of them, is immediately reflected in this light. It does short-sighted psychologists no good to look for symbols or events hidden in the unconscious; they can never free themselves of them. Eroticism everywhere around us suffices to prove that reason does not exhaust the mysterious extent of this order of reality.

There is a fringe of our life which we have a hard time dominating. Each one finds himself in the middle of a debate or a combat. We have the power to complete ourselves in a dialogue with events, things, or beings, in which intermediaries are necessary. But they always pose a question and bring us beyond ourselves and themselves.

We should always concede that things, from the swastika and its violence to Japanese flower arrangements and their mildness, have a meaning for man and that their affective charge ends up surpassing him and themselves.[10] The Nazis were certainly awaiting a savior.

It is a sign of decadence to want to detach symbols from their religious context. We would want to keep all of the flavor and force of ecstasy, so long as they do not end up in something precise.

We have to wake up someday and ascertain that in every domain, reason alone[11] is insufficient to master the meaning of things and beings: "there is nothing so reasonable as this disavowal of reason" (Pascal).

If he wants to find unity in his life, man must accept the intervention of someone who surpasses him. When he refuses this call and this surpassing, he places himself in a state of isolation; we have observed this unfailingly. We do not mean to say that this symbolic part is religious or supernatural. But we mean to say that the religious, the Christian supernatural, comes this far to seek us. God passes through the opening which reality creates and maintains in us. We can say that Christian existence is sacramental only if we go that far. The sacraments act like symbols. But these symbols are not the images of Epinal; they are burning, like fire.

NOTES

1. "In the fight against sin, you have not yet had to keep fighting to the point of death. Have you forgotten that exhortation of God in which you are addressed as sons? 'My son, when the Lord corrects you, do not treat it lightly; but do not get discouraged when he reprimands you. For the Lord trains the ones that he loves and he punishes all those that he acknowledges as his sons.' Suffering is part of your training; God is treating you as his sons. Has there ever been any son whose father did not train him? If you are not getting this training, as all of you are, then you would not be sons but bastards" (Heb. 12:4–11).

2. *Every man is a symbol.* ". . . Léon Bloy's sentence: 'In reality, every man is symbolical; and he is alive to the degree of his symbol.' The word symbol implies a fragmentation or a lack. A symbolic object

is a sign which recalls something else or recalls *to* something else. The thing that I hold in my hand has no meaning for me except in relation to the other thing with which it forms a *whole*. I do not contain myself. If I say *me*, it is because I do not hold myself entirely; this *me* that I hold—and which does not hold me—only regards the whole which I am lacking. . . . The quasi-physical superabundance and the mysterious saturation which I sometimes feel. . . . And it would be the same thing if I were to speak of the indescribable emptiness which takes possession of me quite beyond any agony, the lack in which everything leaves me. The spirit's symbolic vocation is to suffer the abyss of distance and to have a presentiment of fullness" (Pierre Emmanuel, *Le goût de l'un* (Paris: Ed. du Seuil, 1963), p. 39.

"The day when theology has ceased being symbolic and the era of great dissociations has opened for the Christian culture. Now that it has no more contact with the culture which raised it up—Biblical culture—theology is much more radically losing the power to live in symbiosis with every human culture whatever it be, and especially with ancient culture. We can never measure symbols with concepts. The relationship which theology maintains with the literary images (*Weltanschauung*) of an age exactly defines the relationship which theology maintains with the culture of that age. A theology without images is a theology without culture. It is the image which constitutes cultural unity" (Pie Duployé, *La religion de Péguy*, Ed. Klincksieck, 1965, p. XI).

3. Cf. P. R. Régamey, *Portrait spirituel du chrétien* (Ed. du Cerf, 1963), "Voir ce que l'on voit" pp. 147 ff.

"My conviction that no recognition or *encounter* is possible between men on the basis of a Sense which is already there and which it suffices for them to accept. . . . If we are relative beings, it is because we cannot really be what we pretend to be, so long as others cannot see us. Each one of us is separated from the other person and consequently from ourself; and we need the other person's agreement in order to meet him. I cannot recognize, accept, or reconcile myself with myself except to the degree in which I am able to reconcile myself with others. . . . Where can we place the truth of this enterprise of humanization, if not in the very reality of speaking it?" F. Jeanson, *La foi d'un incroyant* (Paris: Ed. du Seuil, 1963), pp. 158–159.

4. *A proliferating abstraction.* "Language is given to us and is ours to *affect* the world and to affect ourselves with all the meaning we can without going out of ourselves. When our spirit no longer listens to its vocation and no longer tends toward the total sense which is its very being, it ceases to take form and is no longer any more than its own matter for ideas. And then it falls into the paradox of divided nature: a proliferating abstraction, which is nothing more than an appearance, vainly opposes itself to the ever increasing weight of matter. The temptation of modern intelligence is to think itself detached from its object and free to modify matter without taking account of our incarnation and our reciprocal relation with the world. Detached, the spirit multiplies the diverse; and it admires its fruitfulness in this and thinks that the idea of unity is sterile" (Pierre Emmanuel, *op. cit.,* pp. 21–22). Cf. Brice Parain, *Recherches sur la nature et les fonctions du langage* (Paris: Ed. Gallimard, 1942); M. Foucault, *Les mots et les choses* (Paris: Ed. Gallimard, 1966).

5. Cf. R. Alleau, *De la nature des symboles* (Paris: Ed. Flammarion, 1958), pp. 11 ff; G. Durand, *L'imagination symbolique* (Paris: P. U. F., 1964), pp. 7–15.

6. Cf. C. Levi-Strauss, *Tristes tropiques* (Paris: Ed. Plon, 1955), pp. 424–427. English trans: *Tristes Tropiques* (New York: Criterion, 1961; Atheneum, 1964).

7. *Marilyn Monroe.* "To participate in a drama is to momentarily identify oneself in a way with the hero of the drama. What relation can this have with us and our problems, difficulties, hopes and despairs, and Marilyn Monroe? It is very simple. If, at the other end of the white telephone that she held in her hand without being strong enough or really wanting to use, you had heard her foggy voice saying: 'I am going to commit suicide,' how would you have been able to object, to offer her some reason to live? This act of suicide makes us dizzy. The proof is that in the United States they are now trying to show that it was an accident. And everyone, as soon as he was informed, came up with a justification for Marilyn Monroe's death, like a defense, paging through her life to hurriedly find an original reason, one which belonged only to her and which does not put into question our system of thought and our way of life. In former times, to live decently we had to love God and make ourselves worthy of being loved

by him. The task was inexhaustible and duty was followed even if not respected. God is dead, and—even though everyone is still invoking him—he is still more dead in the United States than in Europe" (Françoise Giroud, *L'Express,* August 9, 1962).

8. Cf. E. Morin, *Les stars,* Ed. du Seuil, 1957, "Dieux et déesses," pp. 35 ff.; "La Liturgie stellaire," pp. 69 ff.

"We may know nothing about the cave men, but a few bisons painted on the walls by these men speak to us as well today as they did the first day they were painted. Culture is that which, in death, is the same as in life. I offer another example, one so banal that we never think of it: the religious phenomenon. For a Christian, Jesus Christ is not a man who belongs only to a certain age, he is living. For a Buddhist, Budda is not a man belonging to a past time in history, he is present. For all the religions, their prophets are always present. The same is true for a work of art; its fundamental character resides in this mysterious survival. There is a gigantic phenomenon occurring in our civilization which we are hardly noticing. . . . We are always talking about machinism. We forget that a century ago in Paris three thousand Parisians went to the theater every day; now three million and a half Parisians go to see fiction every night. Machines have less power over the soil and human actions than those machines which play upon the mind. . . . After having said so many times that we could not loan *la Joconde* (Da Vinci's *Mona Lisa*) because it could not make the voyage, I was happy when it was finally received in the United States by the President, the Senate, and the Supreme Court as no living being was ever received. And in Washington, a city where the majority are black, I saw women come with their children, their eyes lowered, to raise them to the painting, and then disappear in the crowd. Millions of people came, in a certain way to thank France" (A. Malraux, defining culture, discourse at the Assemblée Nationale, Nov. 1963).

9. Cf. P. Ricoeur, *De l'interpretation. Essai sur Freud,* Ed. du Seuil, 1965; and C. G. Jung, *L'homme et ses symboles* (Paris: Ed. Laffont-Pont-Royal, 1964 (English trans: *Man and His Symbols,* New York: Dell, 1967); and *L'âme et la vie,* Buchet-Chastel, 1965.

10. *To come back to the heart:* Do we sufficiently recognize those who witness to this surpassing? They must often witness in trembling and blasphemy and sometimes even in expressing the limit of madness.

We should not ignore the fact that this research into surpassing is for them a matter of life or death. If some of them expressed their conflicts because they have taken it seriously, the question is posed to everyone. Everyone is asked "to come back to the heart" under pain of having cheated with things, his existence, and God. Nothing can replace loyally listening to the poets. Whatever generation of poets it may be, the "damned," the surrealists, or contemporaries, all have the same eagerness to witness to the opening of the spirit.

"Everything brings us to believe that there exists a certain point in the spirit where life and death, the real and the imaginary, the past and the future, the commensurable and the incommensurable, the high and the low, seeks to be conceived contradictorily. We search in vain for another purpose in surrealist activity than the hope of determination on this point" (*Deuxième manifeste surréaliste*). "Poetry is the testimony of a nature exiled in the imperfect and that wants to possess immediately on this earth a revealed paradise" (Baudelaire). "Poetry is expression by means of human language, brought to its essential rhythm, of the mysterious sense of the aspects of existence" (Mallarmé). "There was a man who was no longer hungry, and no longer ever able to be hungry because he had devoured so many inheritances, gobbled down so much food, and impoverished his neighbor. One day he found his table empty, his bed deserted, his wife fat, and the soil in the field of his heart evil. Not having a tomb and wanting to live, having nothing to give and less to receive, he found that objects fled from him; he stole famine and made himself a plate which became his mirror and his own ruin" (René Char, *Le masque funèbre*).

Let us recall, among the most important poems: Hölderlin's *Hyperion;* Rilke's *Sonnets to Orpheus,* I and III, and the ninth *Elegy of Duino;* Lautréamont's *Chants de Maldoror;* Rimbaud's *Le bateau ivre* and *La saison en enfer;* Mallarmé's *Hérodiade, Igitur,* and *La lettre à Cazalis;* Valéry's *L'ébauche d'un serpent* and *Palme;* Antonin Artaud's *Ombilic des lymbes;* Claudel's *La Catastrophe d'Igitur;* and René Char, Saint-John Perse, Pierre Reverdy, La Tour du Pin, and Pierre Emmanuel.

It is also good to listen to what those who combat with the passion of art have to say: cf. conversations with Matisse, Dali, Manessier, Rouault, Segonzac, Léger, Braque, Lapicque, Bazaine, Giacometti in

G. Charbonnier, *Le monologue du peintre* (Paris: Ed. Julliard, 1959 and 1960; and the *Notes sur la peinture d'aujourd'hui* of J. Bazaine (Paris: Ed. du Seuil, 1953).

Let us recall a few of Chagall's statements: "Perhaps another eye and another view exists, an eye of another order and placed in a different way, not where we are used to finding it. . . . Apollinaire came to find me in my studio. And there, to my surprise, he pronounced the magic word 'supernatural.' Supernatural, he said gasping for breath, himself blushing before the paintings he had not expected. To tell the truth, I little understood the word at that moment, nor what the word 'surrealism' meant.

"A thing must allude to others to acquire its true identity. . . . My entire life is identified with my work, and it seems to me that I am the same when I sleep. . . . My painting has been mocked a lot. I would smile, sadly no doubt, at the meanness of my judges. But I had never-theless given a sense to my life. The thing that has always tempted me the most is the invisible side, the so-called illogical side of form and spirit without which exterior truth is not complete for me.

"Only mine—the country I find in my soul—I enter it without a pass-port—I am home.—It sees my sadness—and my solitude.—It puts me to sleep—and covers me with a perfumed stone. Gardens blossom in me—my flowers are invented. The streets belong to me—but there are no houses. They have been destroyed since my childhood. The inhabitants wander about in the air—looking for lodgings—they live in my soul.

"There are no fairy stories in my paintings, nor fables, nor popular legends. I am against the terms of 'fantasy.' Our entire world is reality, and perhaps still more real than the apparent world. When we call fantasy or fairy story everything that seems illogical to us, we admit that we do not understand nature" (Chagall, exposition au Musée des Arts decoratifs, 1959).

"Men today, carried by the trying rhythm of competition, subjected to mechanical means, no longer have time; and they are in danger of losing their taste for 'coming back to the heart,' as Holy Scripture says. But this is the condition for a true life with God. Priests themselves should 'go back to the heart,' not only to be Christian and finally saved, but to maintain a truly religious and Christian pastoral action which helps others to win salvation. It is on this level, the least 'practical' and nevertheless the most efficacious, that pastoral renewal is situated or should begin" (Y. Congar, Preface to K. Delahaye, *Ecclesia Mater,* Paris: Ed. du Cerf, 1964, p. 15).

11. *With the flesh.* We quote this statement by Jean Renoir: "In the end, when we are really standing at the bottom of the wall, we must kill general ideas. It is perfectly true that when you are thinking about a plan and you say to yourself 'I am going to try to do something enormous; it is going to be the most beautiful plan of my life, the most beautiful plan in movie-making,' well! you are not going to make this plan with general ideas. You will do it with a little burst in your vision. You will do it with details, details that have to do with the flesh, with the senses, with vision, with smell, with the sensual joy of sensing forms and colors; not with ideas or with your brain. The brain is an old prostitute. What does the brain do? It profits from what the other senses have honestly accumulated. It takes it for itself and attributes it to itself. Well! my dear friends, we have to fight against that" (Jean Renoir, "Ce bougre de monde nouveau," in *Les Cahiers du cinéma,* Christmas 1957).

7 Christ and Symbols

Symbols and signs exist in our life. We do not always know where they come from but they are there. We can no more by-pass them than we can a dialogue with everything surrounding us. Does this mean that the universe of symbols and this strife of man and things is automatically religious and supernatural? Does it suffice to be open to other things than oneself to be Christian?

No, it does not suffice for us to liberate or decipher this call in order to find God. On the contrary, there is no worse illusion for man than a gluttony for the sublime and the falsely religious under the pretext of experience.[1] It is not enough that human realities be symbols for them to become Christian sacraments.

Many symbols are blemished, either because they close us in on ourselves and have no other purpose than to nourish our excitement, or because they only distract us by keeping us in a perpetual state of evasion.

But by what right, then, in the midst of the burning dialogue of our life, do certain acts, signs, and symbols take on *religious* value? What will enable us to escape the dream and to avoid a mystique which is nothing but a form of fine art? Among all the different types of invitations, how can we "open the door only to the Unique?" How can we recognize it? And *at the same time,* how can we give it full right and full dynamism and accomplishment through the truest tendencies and symbols of our life?

Wherever we ask, the Bible, the history of religions, Christian practice, psychology, the answer is the same: a reality cannot *become a religious symbol except to the degree in which it expresses an exchange, in which it is the material of a communion.*[2]

The purpose of the Incarnation is not only to manifest an all-powerful God; nor to console us for the fact that we are not God, but to declare to us God's *love* in a real way. God gives God to men. This is more than a doctrine and more than a simple history. On the feast of the Epiphany, the Church sings: "oh admirable exchange!" At Christmas, the Church summarizes its prayer by saying: "deign to accept our sacrifice, so that, in a prodigious exchange, we may become similar to your Son in whom our nature is similar to yours." All the symbols of our existence find their completion and the realities of our life become religious only to the degree that we participate in this exchange.

For every Christian thinker, whether it be St. Paul, St. Thomas Aquinas or the Curé d'Ars, the truth which dominates all of faith is that God, being love, is exchange and communication and participation. And this to an unforeseen degree, "a secret that never enters man's heart by his powers alone."

For the Christian, everything proceeds from the divine goodness and the blessed fruitfulness of God. When it concerns a created, limited being, this communication is a benefit for him who gives himself. He is the first to find his good there, because, for him, to give himself is to win a new existence and to obtain an excess of value and existence. Only when we speak of God, because he is perfect, can we say that his gift is not determined or commanded by anything else than pure generosity. God alone gives without profit, without return.

In another sense, to *be* love means to attract. And here again, in the strict sense of the term, God alone can be a source of attraction. This, because he has not received from another that by which he attracts; and he alone has the right to attract to himself exclusively and jealously without harming the person he is attracting and without fearing to deprive him of a benefit that he might get elsewhere: because God alone is perfect and infinite, and for God alone there is no elsewhere.

We should even say that God's way of giving is to attract to himself and to put creatures in relation with his richness and his perfection; and he is the only one for whom this is true without egoism. God alone is exchange and love. And it is by this exchange with God that we penetrate at the same time the ultimate secret of what he himself is and of what man's highest dignity is.

When we speak of exchange in communion, we are approaching the notion of sacrifice. And this alone enables us to understand how all symbols become religious and leave the imaginary in order to join concrete existence. In effect, when we say that God is love and participation, unless we want to merely stay with words and therefore with a lie and illusion, we have to admit that this Covenant between God and man, this exchange of life, is founded on a reality. Every being that loves knows that it will cost him to love. We cannot love and at the same time want to keep our distance from the one we love. When we offer something through love, even if it is a limited thing, we offer it with our whole heart.

When a Christian reduces the idea of sacrifice to a kind of

market, he blasphemes against God much more than a non-Christian does. When we go to confession, we are not going merely to buy forgiveness for a certain sin or to reconcile ourselves with God because we have committed a certain fault, but we are rather bringing our entire good will to confide it in God so that he can take charge of it. When we get married, we do not sacrifice our independence only to be able to have two or three children, to answer our sexual needs, or to be sure to have someone around to clean up after us, but we are confiding our *entire* life in the other person as in God, for better or for worse. When we share in the bread and wine at Mass, we are not in communion only with this or that friend, but with the entire Mystical Body. When we make a sacrifice, we are not just offering up a privation, but we are manifesting our desire to convert our entire life: "may our works of penance lead to a true conversion of heart," prays the liturgy during Lent.

Every religious act is a real thing, terribly real. In fact, sacrifice is not homage or purely and simply an offering, but an act in which man consecrates his existence and throws it into a fire which comes to consummate his life and to give it a meaning. This sacrifice is the expression of a desire to be taken by God and the sign that man accepts to be completely taken: "not that I have become perfect yet: I have not yet won, but I am still running, trying to capture the prize for which Christ Jesus captured me" (Phil. 3:12).

If it is not to be an illusion, this communion between God and man must be total. But to effect this offering of his life, man cannot without killing himself *give everything at one single time. This is why he needs symbolic intermediaries.* Thus, everything in the life of man which can represent an aspect of his activity, as a symbol, will become religious *by becoming material for sacrifice.*

Every symbol escapes the kingdom of dreams and imagination exactly in the measure it is charged with a new function of entering into the movement of exchange and communion between God and man. Bread and wine will no longer be signs of strength and joy or of the common labor of people; they will become the offerings of this work and joy, accepted by God and returned to men. Patience, fidelity, and passion in love between two beings will no longer be merely the symbol of an affection, but the expression of God's sentiments towards us and of the way he treats us. The very wound of sin and its repentance are no longer merely the sign of failure and of good will, but the sign of God's eternal mercy and youth which comes to us.

The supreme reality of all religious life—union and exchange between God and man in sacrifice—is the departure point for any inquiry as to how the symbol finds its completion. The "sacrifice" is the moment of this mystery which transports man's being into God's being and permits man, in return, to possess God.

There is no such thing as a small sacrifice. Neither is there any sacrifice which is only a privation. Christ came to free us and not to propose a religion of agony. When we recognize that sacrifice is at the heart of every sacrament, this is not to set ourselves on a road of mutilation. Quite the contrary. There is no other road but sacrifice if we want to complete and save all the realities of our life. To refuse it is to close ourselves to every exchange with God, and to close every door to the only life for which we are made.

But we must also repeat that an attitude which sees in sacrifice only the negative aspect of privation and immolation, betrays the best of human life and at the same time betrays God's heart. We cannot speak well of heaven when we condemn the earth. We do not respect God's transcendence when we scorn the Incarnation. We are not spiritual because we are turned away from the temporal. Péguy observes:

It does not suffice to abase the temporal in order to elevate oneself into the category of the eternal. It does not suffice to abase nature in order to elevate oneself to the category of grace. It does not suffice to abase the world in order to elevate oneself to the category of God. . . . Because they are not of man, they think that they are of God. Because they love no one, they think that they love God. But Jesus Christ himself was of man.[3]

Offering, immolation, and even destruction, are essential to sacrifice; but we must add that *there is sacrifice at the moment there is exchange between God and man,* and therefore at the moment that man has recognized God's goodness, because, in order for there to be exchange, I must have recognized the Other and recognized that he gives me something. The soul of every sacrifice is this will for communion which rises in man's heart on the day he recognizes the source of his being and that this source is Someone whose nature is participation and exchange: a God of Love and Trinity.

In this sense, we can say that Christ's life was a sacrifice from the first instant of the Incarnation, because it expressed such an encounter between God and man that man could finally recognize in God the source of all his life and say to him "Our Father." We understand that Holy Thursday and the Mass, Good Friday and the cross, Easter and the Resurrection are the decisive moments in this sacrifice because they express perfectly the definitive exchange between God and man. Therefore, the Christian religion can simultaneously recognize a God who is good, a Father, and be centered on a sacrifice, because the sacrifice is nothing but the *supreme, real expression of the exchange and sharing between man's life and God's life,* a praise, a eucharist to the good God. In this sense, it is not contradictory to admit that the essence of all religion is to be a communion between the creature and God and that the principal religious activity is sacrifice. When the patrician, Perpetua, and her slave, Felicitas, were in the Roman prisons awaiting martyrdom, Felicitas was about to give birth to a child. During childbirth, because she was crying out, one of her guards said to her, "If you cry now, what are you going to do in the amphitheater when the beasts tear at you?"—"Oh," answered St. Felicitas, "then Another will be suffering in me."

In a word, this woman defined the secret of every Christian attitude and summarized St. Paul's intuition: "in your minds you must be the same as Christ Jesus" (Phil. 2:5); "When we were baptized we went into the tomb with him and joined him in death, that as Christ was raised from the dead by the Father's glory, we too might live a new life" (Rom. 6:4); "Never say or do anything except in the name of the Lord Jesus" (Col. 3:17); "It is through him that we answer Amen to the praise of God" (II Cor. 1:20); and finally, "I live now not with my own life but with the life of Christ who lives in me" (Gal. 2:20).

We can believe that the essence of the sacraments is expressed when we say that they work a great recapitulation of the forces and symbols of human life. We think that we said everything when we showed that we must bring the dispersed forces of our life to the domain of the sacred by inscribing them in an exchange and sacrifice. It seems that we can say no more once we have recognized that the sacraments lead us to union with God. *But, it is not the sacred, as sub-*

lime as it is, which makes the gestures of our life Christian.
It is a person: Jesus Christ. The sacraments lead us all the
way to this mysterious substitution of another life for ours.
In each sacrament we are faced with accepting or refusing
Someone. Faced with Christ, we must either flee or allow
Another to take care of us.

Each sacrament poses a question of life or death. Each
represents the decisive aspect of a Passover, the aspect by
which Baptism is at the same time the death of the old man
and the birth of the new, Christ in us. We are reborn because
we have understood that we can no longer live alone. And
each time it is possible for us to accept or refuse life or death
a little more, and, like the Hebrews before they crossed the
Red Sea, we must choose. We cannot lead two lives. If we
accept Christ's life, we must know that it will take over completely and that finally, *without denying anything of our
own,* we will somehow *become* Christ the Son of God.

It is true that if Christ is not living we are the most unfortunate of men and the sacraments will have been only one
more illusion. It is not up to us alone to carry out the sacrifice of our life. It is not by our own action alone that we
must save ourselves. But it is God who has taken the initiative to share our destiny and to invite us to table with his
friends. It is he who has loved us first of all (I Jn. 4:10). It is
he who takes the first step each morning.[4] "For thirty years
I looked for God; and at the end of that time, I realized that
it was he who was waiting for me" (Ansari). The Christian
signs are new precisely in the fact that they indicate to us
this ever free and ever present initiative of the saving God,
Christ. He has set the table for his friends and has invited us.
It is a marvelous reciprocity which we must know how to
discover! All of the newness and originality of Christianity

resides in this ever actual initiative of God through Christ in view of establishing reciprocity of love.

The young man has come again to his well-beloved. He knocks at the door, and a voice from inside asks: "Who is there?" He answers: "It is I." But the voice inside replies: "This house cannot hold you and me." And the door remains closed. And so the young man calls again: "Beloved, it is I, open up, I am here." But the door remains closed. And so the lover retires to the forest, and prays, and fasts in solitude. A year later, he returns and knocks again at the door, and again the voice asks: "Who is there?" And the lover answers: "Beloved, *it is you.*" And then the door opens to let him in (Jalal ed-Din Rumi).

A strange answer, not "I love you" or "I am waiting for you," but a simple affirmation of what is essential to love, reciprocity.

And this is the way it is for the Christian who asks for salvation, who receives the sacraments to find it, and who discovers that he is saved because he already has Christ's presence and because he has become the One to whom God cannot *not* open, his own Son. When St. Paul says that we are called to be incorporated into Christ, he invites us to much more than to a mere imitation of Christ. Faith and the sacraments which are its proclamation do not propose that we encounter Christ as something exterior to us; they propose that we *adhere* to him, live according to his life, assimilate ourselves to all the stages of his history, and live a new and eternal existence. The epistle for Easter morning has no other conclusion than: "you have died, and now the life you have is hidden with Christ in God" (Col. 3:3).

The gift which God asks of us is the gift of his Son to himself, because this is the gift he makes to us, the Holy Spirit himself. God needs our love as he needs his son. He has decided this eternally. Also, when we stop loving God, God in a way loses his Son; and when we return to him, he refinds his Son. We have the very real power of giving him to him in ourselves. If we refuse, there is a giving of the Son to the Father which does not take place, without, however, the eternal gift ever ceasing. "I have called you friends because everything that I have learned from my Father I have told to you." God has only one love, and when he loves he must give this love. The Father wants to relive with us what passes between him and his Son. So long as we have not gone that far, nothing has been said about the sacraments, because we have not gone right to the end of their "Christian" truth.[5]

By means of the sacraments, our sentiments, desires, and sufferings are transformed into the sentiments, desires, and sufferings of Christ; and this is a transformation similar to the one which is accomplished at Mass, the transformation of bread and wine into the Body and Blood of Christ. We remain ourselves, and yet by means of the sacraments a *transubstantiation* occurs. In a way, we acquire a personality which is infinitely higher than ours; we are no longer alone to sing the psalms or to read the Gospel, we are no longer alone to love or to forgive, to listen or to suffer. It is Christ our eternal high priest who lives, forgives, suffers, sings and reads God's plan of love in heaven:

Therefore, of these two (the Church and Christ), everything has occurred as if there were only one person. . . . If they are two in one single flesh, why not also two in one single voice? Let Christ speak then, because in Christ, the Church speaks; and in the Church, speaks Christ. The Head speaks in the Body, and the Body in the Head.[6]

This brings us to discover the concrete movement which governs all Christian life and the first cry which should open each one of our activities: "come, Spirit of God," "come, Lord Jesus, come," "Lord, teach us to pray." *God alone can form the life of his Son in us,* because definitively *only the love of a God can stand before the love of God.* And we can say that we are Christian on the day we can no longer speak to God or act without doing it with and by Christ, knowing that the only face God does not resist is that of his Son. "All baptized in Christ, you have all clothed yourselves in Christ" (Gal. 3:27; and also I Cor. 1:9; Rom. 6:4; and 13:14; Eph. 4:24). This is the principal movement in the Mass, which is the remembrance of the saving mystery, where we address ourselves to God with the very words of his Son: "recalling the Passion of your Son, his Resurrection, and his Ascension, we offer you the perfect victim . . . and through him, with him, and in him we give you glory."

Therefore, Christ is truly our high Priest, as the Epistle to the Hebrews writes of him saying *"that he calls on his Father unceasingly on the behalf of men."* St. John says that he is our "advocate," and what does this mean if not that our Lord is the one who in heaven presents to his Father our praise and adoration, and well as our petitions, weakness, and hope? Christ repeats our very words before God; he takes our poor human words and makes them his. And in this way our prayer, charity, apostolate, poverty, penance, etc. are made absolutely efficacious, because they have become those of Christ.

God could not give men a more excellent gift than to lead them with his Word, by which he created all things, and to unite them to himself as his members, so that he was at the same time Son of God and son of man; one single God with the Father, one single man with men; so that in addressing our prayers to God, we are not separated from the Son, and so that the body of the Son, offering its prayers, is not separated from its head. Thus, our Lord Jesus Christ, the unique Savior of his Body, prays for us as priest; he prays in us as head; and he receives our prayers as our God. Let us therefore recognize that we speak in him and he speaks in us. . . . *Never speak without him, and he will say nothing without you.*[7]

It is never possible to establish ourselves in a definitive proximity to God. We must be invited. The Gospel parables of the nuptial robe, the banquet, and the pretentious guests remind us that this convocation is always new and gratuitous. As one of Newman's friends said, "Grace is new every morning." Who can pretend to have a right to the divine life? It is grace; and isn't this gratuity itself the guarantee of the infinite distance of him who has called us?

And we are right to stand helpless before a God who is source of goodness and who is always "beyond," who alone can decide, and who alone can bestow or impoverish.

Yes, God's proximity is always marked with the fact that we cannot make ourselves masters of it; and his presence does seem fragile to us at times. But this same God has bound his destiny forever with ours. He has decided it eternally. In "delivering" his Son over to us, he at the same time gave us title to be answered. It is up to us to remind him. God could have done no more to assure us of his proximity. It is as though a judge who wanted to prevent himself forever from being impartial made himself prejudiced on the side of the defendants by suppressing all distance between himself and them. "Without beauty, without majesty, a man of sorrows and familiar with suffering, he was despised and we took no account of him" (Is. 53:3–4). And from now on, God cannot condemn himself.

At the center of every religious act, faith reminds me of this step that God took. And my practice will be Christian in the affirmation that God has already answered our prayers, that he to whom we address ourselves has *already* replied. In this, faith gives us the living proof that God's promise is true and that it has been realized by the gift of his Son. We remember St. Paul's extraordinary cry which summarizes all certitude: "after saying this, what can we add? With God on our side, who can be against us? Since God did not spare his own Son, but gave him up to benefit us all, we may be certain, after such a gift, that he will not refuse anything he can give" (Rom. 8:31–32).

How could he still try to bargain with us, when he has already given us his Son who has eternally willed that the center of the Christian mystery be a "eucharistic" memorial and a praise to his goodness and paternity? "You who keep Yahweh mindful must take no rest. Nor let him take rest until he has restored Jerusalem, and made her the boast of the earth" (Is. 62:6–7).

The essential act in prayer and in the sacraments is this reminding God of the gift he has made to us and of the eternal love for which he cannot *not* hear us; it is a "call to holy things" (an obsecration, as theology says), a call to the mysteries which God's grace and mercy have manifested to us.[8] This "obsecration" is present everywhere in the prayers of the people of God: "and now, Lord, God of Israel, *who brought your people out* of the land of Egypt with a mighty hand, with signs and wonders, with great power and with outstretched arm, to win yourself a name renowned today.

. . . do not call to mind the misdeeds of our ancestors, but *remember* instead your power and your name" (Bar. 2:11 and 3:5).

For the prophets, Yahweh is primarily the God-of-the-Exodus, the God-who-has-liberated, and who cannot, because of this, abstain from liberating again. "How can he who has given you his Son not give you his favor now?" This is the sense of the prayers at Mass, as well as all of the Canon. Forevermore, we hold the "memory" of the sacred mysteries which alone give us the certitude of being answered. And this is also the departure-point for every sacramental process: it arises from recognition of God's gift to us and turns toward the Father of our Lord Jesus Christ.

Our Father in heaven gives us his Son and all the mysteries accomplished in his flesh. They are ours. Almighty God, in giving us his crucified Son and in placing the mysteries of his mercy at our disposition, gives us power over himself. Christ's blood is poured out, and it is at my disposition. How can you remain indifferent to the Body of your Son who is the image of your mercy?[9]

The two great documents which have best formulated Christ's role are Chapters four and five of the Book of Revelation and the Epistle to the Hebrews. Claudel's exultation before Gand's mystical Lamb was entirely correct. It is the Lamb, because he is immolated, who is our guide and leader, the source of all Christian life. The Paschal Vigil does nothing more when it brings Christians to pass from darkness to the altar as they follow the paschal candle. We follow the only one who can open the sanctuary doors, because he carries on himself the stigmata of victory and can eternally recall the price to his Father and to men. Who else can alone open the book of human destiny, if not the Lamb?

For you every vision has become like the words of a sealed book. You give it to someone able to read and you say, "Read that." He replies, "I cannot, because the book is sealed." Or else you give the book to someone who cannot read, and you say, "Read that." He replies, "I cannot read" (Is. 29:11–12).

I wept bitterly because there was nobody fit to open the scroll and read it, but one of the elders said to me, *"There is no need to cry: he has triumphed, and he will open the scroll and the seven seals of it."* Then the Lamb came forward to take the scroll from the right hand of the One sitting on the throne, and when he took it, the four animals prostrated themselves before him and with them the twenty-four elders. They sang a new hymn: *"You are worthy to take the scroll and break the seals of it, because you were sacrificed, and with your blood you bought men for God, of every race, language, people and nation"* (Rev. 5:4–9).

Contrary to what we often imagine, attraction to the sacraments comes from above.[10] This is why it is always accompanied by a conversion. It is not a matter of speaking, explaining, or acting, but of listening and receiving. God has preceded us. And we come to recollect the Lamb's life and to make it ours. Only he could open the book; and only he still can. The ultimate reason which founds the sacraments and assures their necessity is that God has wanted to give us his Son as mediator and priest and as the only intermediary worthy enough to save us.

Weeping is not reserved to the author of the Book of Revelation. It should be our part when we try to go to God by our strength alone, each time we do not give the sacraments their true place in our life. The testimony of the saints is significant in this regard. They all give us the example: Joan of Arc followed the liturgical times and their requirements with exactitude, whereas war and captivity had dispensed her from this worry; St. Bernard taught his monks to live according to the moment of the redemptive mystery; Theresa of Avila took care to nourish her interior prayer with it. None of them pretended to have any other milieu of life than the mystery of Christ. "Your face is my only fatherland," said St. Thérèse de Lisieux.

We can summarize what we have written above as follows:

—our life is not a mere *datum;* it is both given and remains to be made.

—we have to complete it through the intermediary of a dialogue with things, that is, through symbols.

—but, for this, we are not alone; in taking them up, Christ has consecrated symbols and the actions of our life.

—our existence becomes incomprehensible, uneasy and disturbing, so long as we have not joined him who alone can open the book of our destiny.

—and it is by means of faith and the sacraments of faith that he proposes to us to do it.

THE SACRAMENTS AND THE SPIRIT
OF POVERTY

Our Lord did not come to replace the bakers, lawyers, and doctors of Palestine with miracles; but, by his actions, he came to rouse the attention of his contemporaries to something which surpassed them: God's intervention. In the same way, the sacraments' role is not to replace the human drama, but rather to address our faith.

We know the story of the painter who drew so perfect a picture of a lion that everyone who saw it was afraid. It was a very bad painting. The purpose of a work of art is to refer us to what surpasses the sensitive, at the very moment it presents us with something. Music, for example, which does not make us feel a fullness that surpasses mere sensitive feeling-good, is mediocre. It does no good to keep playing the same record unless we are merely trying to flee silence and the uneasiness of unquiet desires, and not to comprehend the mysterious reality to which this music brings us.[11] And the same is true for a preacher; we expect not so much a string of intelligent words, but a recalling of the kingdom we have forgotten. The same is true for the liturgy and the sacraments; we do not expect them to fill our senses, but rather to lead us to the silence of a presence and a salvation which comes to us from above.

Two things can be distinguished in every reality which contains a message: the reality itself, and its role as ambassador.[12] We must never forget that it is because of this role as ambassador that the reality interests us. The taste of the bread doesn't matter, when I am asking it to give me Christ.

The purpose of music is not to make me live in sound, though it be harmonized, but to give me a soul. The real problem of the sacraments is not to multiply signs, but to teach us to read those that God has chosen. They teach us to penetrate to the mystery, to the Reality, which the totality of symbols, acts, and stories merely serve. What good does it do to make the flag bigger if I don't know what it represents?

Our contemporaries do not come to the sacraments to ask for a replacement mythology. We should not underestimate either the poetic sense or the transcendent thirst of our companions. They have been able to rediscover a taste for the non-figurative, and they have sufficiently experienced the exasperation which merely sensitive experiences engender, to become allergic to this type of adolescents' food which our liturgical renovations too often offer us. It hardly matters whether we speak of the Exodus or of David and his adulteries, if it is not to read in them living parables of men whom God saved from evil, and if it is not to discover in them explicitly the salvation which has come through Christ in God's name. *What is beyond the signs* commands the understanding of these signs. If we forget the primacy of this "beyond," we prepare misunderstandings and we make the liturgy and the sacraments a process.

Whoever wants "to practice" can never stop requiring a conversion of himself. And this conversion must be one which places what is signified before the sign and refuses to speak of a thing without asking what it has to do with faith. The ultimate reality is what counts here in the first place. The light must not be forgotten; we must make sure that it is present to help us read the meaning of things; the sacraments presuppose faith at the same time as they give it. The minimum demanded for a child to receive Communion is that he be able to know that there is something "beyond" the bread and that he be able to recognize that the first interest in this bread is Christ.

We must go further. The sacraments cannot be reduced to a case of ordinary pedagogy. We must reverse the relationship between the mystery, the principal reality, and the sign which it uses as its messenger.

Not only is it true, as in every work of art, that the most important thing which gives sense to everything else is the work's transcendence, but in the case of the sacraments this transcendence of the sign is a living person, Christ who is God.

When we look at a painting or listen to a symphony, we may be able to participate in "beauty" or in "music," but neither one nor the other is someone. The painting exists and is beautiful, but it does not exhaust beauty. No one has ever encountered "beauty." In the same way, it is not "music" which decides to be interpreted in this or that way.

The contrary is true of the sacraments, because God came before his ambassadors. It is the Spirit of God who chose certain events and not others to carry his message and to re-present the salvation brought by Christ.

It is also he, and he alone, who can give us the key to them. And this is a reversal of all human pedagogy. Only God can give us an eye capable of discerning what there is there to understand, since it is he who has decided it. If this new vision, animated by God at every instant, does not exist, there is nothing left to understand or to "hold together" in the exact sense of the word "sym-bol." Our Lord himself affirmed this solemnly: "then the disciples went up to him and asked, 'Why do you talk to them in parables?' 'Because,' he replied, 'the mysteries of the kingdom of heaven are re-vealed to you, but they are not revealed to them. . . . They look without seeing and listen without hearing or under-standing' " (Mt. 13:10–13; Lk. 8:10). Therefore, by means of my actual and interior sharing in the Spirit of God, I must hold the totality of the mystery which gives to me and hides from me the sensible reality I see.

Do we think that Christ's exclusion, "They look without seeing," applies only to unbelievers? What practical atheism, what absence of faith sometimes accompanies our celebration of the sacraments!

Comparison of the Old and New Testaments helps us to understand why we are sometimes so dissatisfied with the sacraments. Before the time of Christ, religious gestures were principally symbols, figures of a reality to come, something that was accepted. When we read the descriptions of the Old Testament ceremonies, we are surprised at all the apparatus of gestures and rites which accompanied cult, to the point that sometimes they seem like slaughter or the evocation of trances. But it was their normal function to stimulate and excite and unchain as much as possible the desire and call of the human heart. They had to evoke and speak as warmly and dionysiacally as possible. And this was not without danger; men were often quick to take pleasure in the means and to make them the end.

Compared to those of the Old Testament, the signs and sacraments of the New Testament appear to be much more sober. There is no longer the orgy of animal sacrifices, but the sacrifice of bread and wine; no longer the exaltation of initiation rites, but the water of Baptism; etc. We can feel a strange discretion. The sacraments of the New Law are discreet; but their role is no longer to excite us, but rather to bring us a reality. The sacraments possess the reality; they propose to us the fullness of salvation not for the future, but already accomplished and perfected by Jesus Christ.

They give imagination its necessary, concrete, and historical part; but they immediately invite us to surpass by means of faith whatever can be offered on this level and ask us to renounce any trance or exultation which would exist no more than on the level of the senses.

This dispossession at the heart of prayer was necessary, and so was this poverty in spirit which is the first beatitude. How could we be disciples of the Greatest of Poor Men, if we were not poor even in our relations with him and if our prayer itself were not stripped of us, to let his prayer rise up in our hearts, like the cry of our adoption: Abba, Father! (M. Zundel).

There is not only a difference of degree between the signs of the Old and New Testaments, but also *a difference of nature:* the New Testament signs are not oriented towards imaginative excitement, but towards love and the real presence of a person. There is symbol, but this symbol cannot play its role only in virtue of the laws of human psychology. From this viewpoint, it does not function at all, or only incompletely; it hardly evokes, and can even seem weak, like the manna. The sacrament is not only an archetype or a symbol of existence; it is the sign of a presence that is comprehensible only by faith.

As for me, I hear that Christ has been crucified, and I immediately admire his love for men; the pagan also hears it, and he thinks that it is pure foolishness. . . . The pagan who knows about Baptism thinks that it is only water; I do not think only of what I see, I contemplate the soul's purification brought about by the Holy Spirit. The pagan looks at Baptism as a simple washing of the body; I believe that it also makes the soul pure and holy, and I think of the burial, resurrection, sanctification, justice, redemption, the adoption of sons, the heavenly inheritance, the kingdom of heaven, and the gift of the Holy Spirit (St. John Chrysostom).[13]

The sacraments are rooted in our existence; they are not merely the great poetic reference-point of our life, nor are they only the archetype of the battle instinct, of sacrifice, of healing, or of communion. They are God's very life in us, the new actuality of Christ's history, so long as man gives up his taste for what excites him and his imagination accepts the price of obscurity; "praestet fides supplementum, sensuum defectui"—faith supplies for the inadequacy of our senses. The sacraments are in faith. And to keep our taste for them we must always be on our knees. It takes time, faithfulness, and courage, to continue to believe that the sun that has set will give us the stars.

NOTES

1. *Concerning the ambiguity of the sacred.* It is not a matter of backing up and going against one of our most profound convictions, namely, it is not by scorning the temporal that we discover the spiritual; but we must nevertheless be very firm on the equivocal aspects of the sacred: (a) There is a *human* sacred, which we can never go too far in respecting. (b) Just because there are deformities of this sacred, we should not fear or condemn it. (c) But neither should we forget that "the fish begins rotting by the head," that is, the greater a reality is, the more we can be drunken or foolish with it. The worse aberrations come from confusing this human sacred with the religious sacred and from an equivocal looking for the latter in the manifestations of the former. We will cite only one example, the Gurdjieff case: cf. L. Pauwels, *Monsieur Gurdjieff* (Paris: Ed. du Seuil, 1954); P. R. Régamey, in *La Vie spirituelle*, May 1955, pp. 515–517 and July 1955, pp. 5–24; B. Bro, "Les duperies de la foi," in *La Vie spirituelle*, December 1960, pp. 476 ff. (d) We recall in the two following chapters that it is "in the name of Christ" and not only of the holy that we become Christian.

"Religious paganism has also tried to give an exterior form to its interior expectation." On this important question which gives the underlying basis to this chapter, cf. E. Schillebeeckx, *Christ, the Sacrament of the Encounter with God* (New York: Sheed & Ward, 1963), p. 16: St. Thomas, following the line of a long previous tradition, speaks of "natural sacraments" in which he recognizes a real supernatural element. Basing himself on the *Third Book of the Sentences* and the *Summa theologica*, Schillebeeckx shows that St. Thomas admits a "pre-Christian" human sacramentality and, attaching this natural religiosity to God's general salvific will, that it could contain a real supernatural element. We must not categorically reject this element in the "pagan mysteries" because of its deformations or extravagances, as some theologians do, nor put it on the same footing with Christian cult, as some historians of religions have done. But we can consider this human cult in general as the anthropological basis of Christian cult. Cf. E. Lesimple, *Le pressentiment chrétien dans les religions à mystères* (Paris, 1942).

With regard to the Sacrifice of the Mass, the Council of Trent mentions the conformity of this visible sacrifice with the exigencies of man's nature (session XXII, chapter 1; Denz. 938).

On the problem of the sacred with regard to the Christian sacraments, cf. E. Schillebeeckx, *De sacramentale heilseconomie*, pp. 52–59; the short but very suggestive reflections of A. Ayfre in *Le cinéma et le sacré*, "7e art," Paris, 1953, pp. 113 ff.; and P. Ricoeur's conclusions in *De l'interprétation* (Paris, 1966), pp. 504–510.

We also recommend the following studies: L. Gardet, *Expériences mystiques en terres non-chrétiennes* (Paris, 1953), and *Thèmes et textes mystiques. Recherche de critères en mystique comparée* (Paris: Ed. Alsatia, 1958), and in collaboration with G.-C. Anawati, *Mystique musulmane* (Paris: Ed. Vrin, 1961); as well as O. Lacombe, *Chemins de l'Inde et philosophie chrétienne* (Paris: Ed. Alsatia, 1956); and the collective work: *La mystique et les mystiques* (Paris: Desclée de Brouwer, 1966), with H. de Lubac, K. Hruby, H. Jaeger, I. Hausherr, O. Lacombe, J.-A. Cuttat, *et al.* This last work shows the immense territory that has recently been covered by Catholic theology in order to better situate the Christian sacred, thanks to the quality of the works of the pioneers cited above and the decisive impulse permitted and wanted in this domain by the Council.

2. For this entire chapter, we refer the reader to Mircea Eliade's analyses, and especially: *Le sacré et le profane* (Paris: Ed. Gallimard, coll. "Idees," 1965, with bibliography. English trans: *The Sacred and the Profane*. New York: Harper, 1961); *Traité d'Histoire des Religions* (Paris: Ed. Payot, 1949); *Images et symboles. Essais sur le symbolisme magico-religieux* (Paris: Ed. Gallimard, 1952. English trans: *Images and Symbols*, New York: Sheed & Ward, 1961), and *Mythes, rêves et mystères* (Paris: E. Gallimard, 1957). And see the works of E. Schillebeeckx, whose major intuition lies here.

3. C. Péguy, *Note conjointe sur Monsieur Descartes* (Paris: Ed. Gallimard).

4. *"You who loved us first,* Oh God—we speak as if you were the first to love us only once, historically, whereas you never cease to love us first during the course of days and an entire lifetime. When we awaken in the morning and turn our soul toward you, you are first: you have loved us first. If I rise at dawn and immediately turn my soul and my prayer towards you, you are ahead of me, you have loved me first. When I return from distraction and recollect my soul to think of you, you are first. And it is always this way; and we talk like ingrates, as if only once you had been the first to love us" (S. Kierkegaard, *Prayers*).

5. *Charity and reciprocity.* We think that we are still far from having exhausted all of the Johannine richness in this idea. Cf. "Prière ou charité," in *La Vie spirituelle,* January 1960, especially pp. 143–145, 149–150, and 179; A. Feuillet, *Etudes johanniques,* Desclée de Brouwer 1962, cf. Chpt. 3, pp. 126–129 (reprinted in *Le Discours sur le pain de vie,* "Foi vivante," 1967) (English trans: *Johannine Studies,* Staten Island, N.Y: Alba House, 1965). St. Thomas, in a stroke of genius, gave a theological and anthropological formulation to this Biblical proposition, conceiving of charity as friendship. Beyond the hesitations of theologians who preceded him, and in audaciously defining charity as friendship, he is careful to state at the same time that what properly characterizes friendship is *reciprocity* (founded on an exchange and sharing) *in love itself:* in this case, sharing in the good (knowledge, love, happiness) of the divine Persons (cf. II–II, q.23, a.1). And it is this reciprocity which best enables us to explain the unity of the two commandments. Recognition of the role of interpersonal relation, by human sciences, is of primary importance for the analysis and expression of this mystery.

6. Saint Augustine, *In Psalm.* 30:4.

7. Saint Augustine, *In Psalm.* 85:1.

8. We should reread the admirable prayers in Ex. 32:11–14; 34:6–9; Judith 4:9–15; 9:2–14; I Chron. 16:8–16; Ps. 105 and 106; Esther 4:17f–17g; 4:17m–17r; Deut. 9:18, 26; Is. 63:7–19; Jer. 32:20–22; Bar. 2:11; 3:5. Cf. St. Thomas, II–II, q. 83, a. 17 and q. 90, a. 1, ad 3.

9. Saint Thérèse de Lisieux said, "I do not want to let this precious blood be lost! I will spend my life collecting it for souls" (*Novissima*

verba, p. 107). Also cf. the episode related at the beginning of chapter five in *Histoire d'une âme*, or *Manuscrits autobiographiques*, p. 109.

10. Cf., for example, E. Peterson's suggestive study, *Le livre des anges*, Paris, 1954; and the study by J. Tyciak, *Maranatha*, Bonn, 1949.

11. It is perhaps difficult to express this better than has Selma Lagerlöf in the awesome scene of despair of Gösta Berling and the Cavaliers, *Gösta Berling* (Paris: Je sers, 1940). English trans: *The Story of Goesta Berling* (New York: Signet Books, 1962, paper).

12. For theological precisions, the reader should refer to analyses of the distinction between "sacramentum" and "res." Cf. among others, H.-M. Féret, "Sacramentum, res, dans la langue théologique de saint Augustin," R.S.P.T., 29 (1940), pp. 218–243.

13. *In I Cor.*, hom.I, n.7; PG 61, col. 65.

8 Can We Do Without the Liturgy?

Though he be the most powerful man on earth, a man cannot baptize himself. Though he be the Pope, he cannot give himself forgiveness. It is by means of his brothers, visible signs of God, that the Christian receives the sacraments. All of the Church's present reflection and its concrete life—as the Council has magnificently shown us—has set great value on this truth: since the time of the Ascension, Christ's presence, his Body, has been confided to the human community. Man does not save himself alone. It is the "People of God" which is saved.

When, in the middle of her agony, her judges tried to shake Joan of Arc by opposing her love for Christ to her attachment to the Church, she answered, "I believe that Christ and the Church are only one, and that there can be no difficulty in this." And it was from those who condemned her and betrayed the Gospel, that she awaited the Body of Christ, because they were, in spite of all, the Church. It is this same attachment to the Church which explains the veneration that Francis of Assisi or the Curé d'Ars had for priests: "If I were to meet a priest and an angel, I would salute the priest before saluting the angel. The latter is the friend of God, but the priest takes his place."

The symbols of our life can become rich not only in consolation, but with saving power, to the degree that they transmit to us Christ's energies. But the sacraments incorporate us into Christ only by attaching us to the Church. Therefore, we will now inquire into the necessity of this relationship.

It is not always easy for new graftings which contain new sap to tolerate their attachment to an old trunk. We cannot speak about the sacraments without evoking the real sacrifice demanded of a man of good will simply to accept and even to understand the language of the liturgy and of clerics.

"While they bray like donkeys in their churches and sing psalms which they number without understanding them, they think that they are making the heavenly persons happy" —thus wrote Erasmus of the clerics.[1] It is not only lately that the Church's prayer and its admirable liturgy and its assemblies have attracted sarcasm. To be sure, he may have had a number of reasons for aiming his arrows at the sixteenth century Franciscan and Dominican friars, but we cannot be satisfied with our worship merely because we have carried it out together.

Before examining all our difficulties and insufficiencies, we must affirm as clearly as possible why all salvation and union with God is real for a Christian only to the degree that he is attached to the community of his brothers. To be incorporated into Christ is to be incorporated into the assembly of the Body of Christ. When we look to the sacraments, we are necessarily looking to a collective salvation.

Let us take a look at the reasons which come both from earth and from heaven, which explain to us the place which the Christian assembly occupies in sacramental practice.

Every living being needs a milieu in which to develop. The

most insignificant things, a disturbance in the atmosphere, a change in the weather, can destroy life. A spring freeze or a sudden drop in temperature during May can destroy the harvest. The same is true for what is most precious and most fragile in man, his divine life. He cannot breathe in just any atmosphere. There are lands without sun and lands without heat which leave only a desert in the soul. Every man needs a home so that his life can be born and develop, an environment in which he can learn to act according to the ways of Christ. This milieu is the Church assembly and its liturgy.[2]

In the same way as man does not invent his life, he does not invent his faith; he receives it. In the same way as he has not invented his salvation, but receives it from Christ, he receives life from the Spirit of God, already given to the community of the children of God. This requires an education. And a very exact pedagogy is proposed to us through the unfolding of an existence, a history that never ends, lived by a man, Christ. This history has become eternal because he was the Son of God.[3]

The sacraments are not episodes independent from one another; salvation has not been given to us under the form of nourishing rations which are occasionally delivered to us by parachute. The ministers of the sacraments cannot be like automatic distributors. We are invited to enter into an existence which has its coherence and its history. Preoccupation with an ideal is not the first thing we must be concerned with; rather, the first thing we must do is cooperate in a work whose initiative comes from Another.

We must learn to place ourselves in relation to another's desires and accept taking part in a project that is older than we are. This is why we all have to be initiated into this plan and receive it from those who have preceded us in the journey of the People of God. Each generation educates and brings the following one into this movement of life, once it is born of Christ and is sustained by expectation of him.

And it does not suffice to assimilate the liturgy like village folklore, or community traditions, or the customs of a family or profession. No, the liturgy is a living milieu, indispensable, that the man who wants to live his faith may breathe, grow, and be nourished. And if the milieu disappears, life does also.

It is possible to give many examples of the confusion a person feels after he has been transplanted or uprooted. This confusion is welcome when it obliges us to deepen the reasons for faith and practice and to decipher (or bring into existence) truer conditions for prayer and the sacraments in the new milieu. But experience proves that for that we must re-create the minimum atmosphere necessary for the Christian life.

In one way or another we all know a kind of uprooting. For many of us, it is perhaps only on that day that we learn to look at the Church with truth and at the liturgy and the assembly of our brothers with the mercy and affection we should always have.

Let us consider a few limited examples: the seminarians who were drafted into the French army during the Algerian war all discovered after a while the radical insufficiency of their good will. They were, indeed, "professionals" in religious practice and prayer; but the seminary program no longer assured their faithfulness, nor did any exterior rule they might impose on themselves. In the middle of the war, in the most diverse situations, as accountants, chauffeurs, radiomen, quartermasters, secretaries or teachers, or fighting in the front lines, all knew confusion and temptation. Only to the degree in which, under the pressure of events, there grew the beginnings of an "assembly" or a "team" (though it be with only one other person), were the true reasons for the sacraments rediscovered; and this, only to the degree in which they consented to experience their confusion to its depths.

Algeria places the priest in the middle of a real paradox and in an often tragic tension. He is a man of peace who is now organizing war; he is the man who preaches love now shooting a gun and telling others to do so; he is the man of God confronted with the scorn and torture of man.

We first of all suffer isolation. We know that we are united to the Church, but when we are in rough country without Mass, the sacrament, or contact even with an overworked chaplain, and without the support of a group of Christians, we quickly find ourselves becoming unfaithful. War does as much harm to those who wage it as to those who suffer it.

These last days, action has been intense and the corner we are in is dangerous. I think that the most important thing I have learned here is to live in community. The Christian who is alone or who lives alone in his own corner has a hard time holding himself up. One day he will find himself submerged. We all need to be "told off" sometimes in order to make a fresh and better start. The service is a good chance to discover the other person. A person has to know how to be quiet and how to listen to his friends.

All of these remarks emphasize that just as there cannot be Christian practice without a milieu and an assembly, reciprocally there can be no assembly without a personal relationship of each person to Christ. And this supposes a fidelity which requires heroism:

Piled into a barracks with hardly room to walk between the beds, we cannot help finding the atmosphere heavy, whether because of the noise, blaring radios, or drinking bouts. And hearing people whining doesn't uplift the soul; the biggest distraction is getting one's face pushed in. As for personal prayer . . . we have to join it to the question of silence and courage. It is especially when we are on guard-duty, or during a pause in the course of an operation, that I can pray. And then it suffices to hear and especially to see what is going on to understand the real meaning of the words, *Peace, Justice,* and to address myself to God, who is Peace, Justice.

At the beginning I thought that prayer rose up almost naturally sometimes. But I quickly noticed that that is not sufficient, or rather that we quickly lose the habit and the taste for taking advantage of these occasions. I felt the need to plan certain times in the day when I would pray; and I had to hold myself to them absolutely. The ideal time seems to be night guard-duty. I have one or two hours of it every night. I decided to spend that time praying instead of just dreaming.[4]

We find the same reality in a document published under the title, *Letters from Stalingrad.* They are letters which were on the last plane able to leave Stalingrad at the end of the battle. This mail was confiscated by the German army and later rediscovered. The soldiers who were writing to their loved ones knew that there was nothing left for them except death or imprisonment. At such a time, the assembly, the feeling of being bound to a common body, that of Christ, takes on all its force; and what a lesson this is for our little parish quarrels or our spats over persons or principles! These men were waiting for two things that they could have never deserved alone and which only the assembly could give them: forgiveness for their sins and the Body of God.

Along with the letters of a displaced soldier, a general's son to his father, a pastor's son, a pianist whose fingers are frozen, we read the letter of a priest who gathered together a few men to celebrate Midnight Mass:

. . . The night before Christmas, eleven of us celebrated Christ's birth inside a little cabin more or less intact. It was not easy to find them among the flock of deceived, hopeless, and doubting men. But those I found came because they wanted to. There are many altars in our vast world, but there certainly is none poorer than here! Right up until yesterday, shells were piled on the box on which I today spread the gray-green tunic of a companion fallen in combat. I read extracts from the Gospel according to St. Luke. I gave them communion under the form of black bread, representing the Body of our Lord and, for them, I implored his grace and mercy. But I did not speak of the fifth commandment. . . . The boys were seated on pieces of wood, and their eyes were raised to me. . . .[5]

Every living being is responsible for his milieu. The strong must care for the weak. And the same is true for Christian practice; this is what the Credo calls the communion of saints.

Therefore, the meaning of the liturgy and the reason for common life and common prayer can be summarized as follows: the Church offers us Christ's energies and welcomes us into the living milieu in which these energies can blossom forth. Just as a member cannot live detached from the body, so also a Christian cannot do without the community. We are Christian only if we are members of Christ; and in this way we allow life to come into us by communion with the faith and activity of our brothers. The Council has given us vivid testimony of this: all the bishops admitted that the fact of living together and praying together had worked a real conversion in them. The lesson was so strong that they vowed they could never forget it and that this had created something irreversible in the life of the Church. The difference between the third and the first sessions was for many the proof that they had not suspected to what point this common prayer modified their conduct.[6]

The sons of God are the body of the unique Son of God; and because he is the head and we are the members, there is only one single Son of God. For this reason, he who loves God's sons loves the Father. And no one can love the Father without loving the Son; and whoever loves the Son should also love the sons of God . . . and in loving them, he himself becomes a member in the union of the Body of Christ, and there is only one single Christ loving himself (St. Augustine).

This is what we have to remind anyone who doubts the importance of the liturgy.[7] The liturgy is the irreplaceable educator of our life, exactly in the way that Christ's life is for each of us the ultimate law. No one can do without this education which accompanies us all during the course of our life as the intermediary chosen by God through which to join us.[8]

Christ himself has given us the example: he recognized the cult given to God in the Temple (Lk. 2:46; Mt. 23:21; Mk. 11:17; Jn. 2:15–17). He took part in the assemblies of the Synagogue (Lk. 4:15–17; 13:10; Jn. 8:20; 18:20). He consented to belong to a real community when he recognized the traditions and customs of Jewish cult in its ritual meals, priesthood, and liturgical authority. Our Lord accepted this cult interiorly, not only exteriorly, as the spontaneous reactions of his prayer constantly show us. Thus, on every great occasion of his life, Christ repeats the psalms he learned and received from the community: at the time of his passing triumph (Mt. 21:4), the solemn announcement of his death (Jn. 12:27), at the Last Supper in face of betrayal (Jn. 13:18), in his final discourse (Jn. 15:25) and the final prayer (Mt. 26:38; 27:46), etc.

In the same way, the primitive Christian community remained connected with the Temple (Lk. 24:53; Acts 2:46; 3:3; 5:25, 42; etc.) and maintained all the Jewish uses which had taken on a definitive meaning since Jesus had taken them up.[9]

We condemn ourselves to not being able to understand Christian practice when we ignore the way it is bound to a community and a liturgy—that is, in the proper sense of "the-work-of-a-people"—*such as Jesus accomplished and lived it in his mystery*. We therefore no longer have a choice; Christ has chosen for us. Our holding back from the assembly almost always conceals more serious refusals than mere laziness or individual self-interest. Underneath there are a false angelism, the illusion of believing that we can dispense with learning and receiving from others the nourishment of our life, and finally a refusal of God's will.

As the milieu of life and teaching, is the liturgy reduced to human pedagogy? Actually, human pedagogies, especially of the intellectual order, do not necessarily accomplish what they teach; it does not suffice to follow courses in school in order to become intelligent. A professor may serve as intermediary as well as he possibly can, so that each student may come to the light himself. But the liturgy is much more than night-school. The originality of the Christian mystery comes from the fact that *the sacraments have the power to create what they announce.*

Christ's physical presence announced the message of his Father's mercy in a living way and realized it for those who met him. They could touch his cloak and be cured, look at him and be freed from their spiritual blindness, and pray to him and be saved from their sins. He was "Rabbi," master, doctor, Lord.[10]

Had Christ not been present as a sign, the visible sign of God, neither Mary Magdalen, nor the paralytic, nor the man born blind would have been cured and forgiven. In the same way, our liturgy cannot cause or accomplish anything of the mystery of salvation unless there is a presence, a visible sign.

This sign can no longer be Christ's living humanity as people met him on the roads of Galilee. When our Lord lived among men, he totalized the divine presence. Since the Ascension, we cannot meet him in the same way, because he no longer stands before our eyes. Now, we rediscover this presence in his Mystical Body by means of which life is offered to us. The means of salvation are now entrusted to the assembly of men who pray to God in the name of his Son and who are responsible for the Eucharist. The saving signs can have real force only if this assembly exists.

As reduced as it may be, the assembly is indispensable for all the sacraments, although in a different way for each one; this presence of others is much stronger than we may often think. Not only can I not give myself Baptism or absolution any more than the Anointing of the Sick, the priesthood, or Confirmation, but a marriage is invalid if it does not have witnesses, and a priest does not have the right to celebrate Mass in a church with locked doors. Our customs with regard to Baptism are finally beginning to change[11]; we are beginning to feel how abnormal it is to celebrate it off to the side, and we are returning to the custom of the primitive Church which was to confer Baptism during the Easter Vigil with the catechumens surrounded by the entire assembly, the litany of the saints in heaven, and the communion of "saints" on earth. This presence of others is also recalled to us by the custom which exists in their houses of not letting a Religious die alone; all his brothers are called to be around the dying person, as in baptism.

This communal aspect of Christian cult is not simply a complement which came about more or less accidentally. It is the necessary milieu for the existence of any kind of life. The assembly of my brothers is the "sacrament" which forevermore takes the place of Christ's presence. It is this assembly which transmits faith in the celebrated mystery to me and which holds and regulates the traditions of this faith. It is this assembly which assures my conversion and makes me give the other person, whoever he may be, real attention. The assembly confirms my reconciliation with God by presenting to me the power of this pardon to unite men. The assembly elevates human thanksgiving, by demonstrating that love is stronger than any division. The assembly accomplishes ultimate human justice, by consecrating to God what is produced by the outward activity of men as a decisive sign of their interior desire.

When he proposed to unite us, Christ did much more than bless man's natural desire for community. We said above with regard to dialogue that it is one of the *deepest needs* of human life and one which the clergy runs the greatest risk of misrepresenting. Too often, we stop midway and do not give all its meaning to the assembly which Christ has come to convoke.

To be sure, the reasons given above are perfectly valid: the assembly, milieu of life, is the sign of Christ. But we have to follow the logic of what we are saying, because common life is not always easy or pleasant. "Hell is the others," is too often true for us to content ourselves with answering with impressions as legitimate as they are fleeting, for example, the elation at being united together for Easter or of having sung a psalm in common. Neither does it suffice, in face of all the misunderstandings which occur among Christians, to affirm that we agree with Christ's words.

To understand just how far the assembly goes as the sign of Christ and just how far the sacraments bring us, and in order to overcome all temptations to division, dissension, and disagreement, we have to acquire quite another idea of what the communion of the faithful is than the idea we now hold.

It is not merely a question of what we "do," but of what we "are." And we can never finish discovering to what a surprising degree we are made to share.

It is certain that our spirit is made not only to understand, communicate, share, and open itself to what is, but also that it *is*, by its essence, openness and communion. "To know is to be what is lacking to everything else."[12]

The pebble is what it is and nothing more; it is condemned to remain closed in on itself. Indeed, material things somewhat escape their limitations by means of movement and action: fire seizes the roast, and the plant takes light, but it transforms it into itself because there is room in the fire or the plant only for itself.

With the spirit, a threshold is crossed. Man is himself, but his intelligence is capable of knowing. It has enough power and amplitude to receive in itself something other than itself. I can hold in myself something other than myself without being physically modified by it and without modifying it. Wood may not take the temperature of fire without becoming warmer; but I can know the heat of boiling water without being warm. To know an apple, it is not necessary to become round and red. We can understand, listen to, and meditate on the worries of someone we love, respecting him completely, without hurting his life, what he is, or what he decides. As perfected as calculating machines are, they can never go outside of themselves to read the result. The nobility of the human spirit is that it really is made to grasp everything, and to be communion, and to know.

And yet, man remains blocked by the limitations of his body even if knowledge brings him the remedy for every limitation; this is his greatness and misery.

Does the type of sharing which the spirit and knowledge permit suffice to express the communion of the sacraments?

Christ unites us in the image of the assembly of all creatures in God. Unlike us, God does not have to know realities which remain exterior to him. He does not need to go from one to the other to hold things or persons. Everything which exists receives strength and life from his existence: "through him all things came to be, not one thing had its being but through him. All that came to be had life in him." In him, *everything* is united. He is the mystery of three Persons living in one single God, one single happiness, with whom we communicate on earth. The son in front of his father, and the artist in front of his work give us some understanding of this.

The exchange and communion realized in us by the sacraments means that we are *images of God*. The energies of the Son of God have been given to us to bring this "assembly" together. It is not merely a matter of knowing, of communicating by means of our sensible powers, the singing, the success of the spiritual unity of a ceremony; it must recapitulate creation in its entirety. This is what being "catholic" means. "He has let us know the mystery of his purpose, the hidden plan he so kindly made in Christ from the beginning to act upon when the times had run their course to the end: that he would bring everything together under Christ, as head, everything in the heavens and everything on earth" (Eph. 1:9–10). Communion with all other men—and even with everything good that God has created—is inscribed in man, the image of God, like an exigency, vocation, and need, as well as a tendency and possibility.

The assembly to which the sacraments give occasion does not merely group together things and minds, but everything which is God's image, and in no other way than in the image of God. This reality changes the very nature of our communion. Grains of wheat are entirely transformed when they have been crushed together with water, leaven, and fire, and they make bread. Don't we also sometimes need to be crushed to enter into communion with our brothers?

The assembly of the Body of Christ which the sacraments realize goes much deeper than we might imagine. But we certainly are tempted to doubt it often from what we see before our eyes. So many particularities, dividing attitudes, and dissensions subsist even in the way of celebrating the sacraments themselves! And yet, we cannot dare to say that at some time a reflection of unity has not pierced through. The voting at the Council—which was always preceded by Mass—testifies to this.

We perhaps forget that this unity does not come only from below, from the nostalgia of men, but that it comes from *above,* from him alone who can accomplish it. It is only with the eyes of Christ that we can see this communion; we will see it only on the last day, after the final combat. For now, we are asked to believe in it and to hope in it, because we have the signs: the Eucharist and the assembly of the faithful. Christ handed himself over, he truly *handed over* his Body and his Blood for the Covenant: "this cup is the new covenant in my blood which will be poured out for you" (Lk. 22:20). "The blessing cup that we bless is a communion with the blood of Christ, and the bread that we break is a communion with the body of Christ. The fact that there is only one loaf means that, though there are many of us, we form a single body because we all have a share in this one loaf" (I Cor. 10:16–17).

We have to go still farther. Not only has Christ accomplished this unity, but he *already is* this unity. "God is all in all" (I Cor. 15:28). This terminus of human history and this call before us are possible only because they have already been accomplished *before* us. The Church is a people to gather together and a temple to construct by means of the cement of the sacraments, but it is already gathered together and already constructed. It is not Christ *and* his members, the hierarchy *and* the faithful, the Apostles *and* their successors; it is Christ at his work of recapitulation and lordship bringing everything to unity. "You have put all things under his feet, and made him, as the ruler of everything, the head of the Church, which is his body, the fullness of him who fills the whole creation" (Eph. 1:22–23).

There remains the fact that we are part of a people whose march towards unity is very slow. There remains the fact that the liturgy's power sometimes seems slight compared to the nostalgia of men and their combats and progress for understanding and unity of the human race.

Although the Church assembly should be a perpetual sign to remind men that the unity to which they are called goes much farther than they think, and although the Church is the eternal refuge for all the despairing and deceived who believe in a possible understanding between men, it is no less true that we all have to learn from the efforts which men are exerting to unite themselves. We might easily point out the disappointments in socialism or accuse men of having lost a sense for the divine paternity. It is true that we cannot be brothers if we do not recognize ourselves as sons of one same Father.[13] But do we know how to recognize the immense call to the Gospel and the sign-posts to Christ's life which are found in all the attempts, even the most modest and apparently profane, which men are making to unite themselves?[14]

When we look at the slow and moving rediscovery of the fact that all men have one same destiny, and the fight against all racism (and here, "the border between the kingdom of good and the kingdom of evil passes through our heart," as St. Francis de Sales said), do we consider them foreign to the Christian assembly? Don't the sacraments go that far to seek us? Don't they oblige us to hope against every hope that the divisions are not insurmountable? Haven't the Eucharist and the sharing of bread been given to us to help us better to believe that in every man there is a secret depth at which he can say "Our Father," and through which he can thus take part in the unique assembly, that of the Body of the unique Son, the first-born of the multitude of his brothers?

Who can dare place a limit on this assembly? We should not run too quickly to the allusions in Scripture about the small number of the chosen, because it speaks above all of the immense multitude of all nations and the great number of those who follow Christ.[15]

It took us more than a hundred years to understand that we are concerned by the cry which humanity raised, "proletariat of all nations, unite." And this same humanity asked for no more than to hear a Pope call for peace on earth—*Pacem in terris*—calling together with love "all men of good will," and to hear another Pope say to the assembly of United Nations, "Jamais plus la guerre, jamais plus (Never again war, never again)." But we should also not forget that in the name of the Eucharist the massacre of St. Bartholomew's Day took place.

REFORMS, BUT ALSO DIFFICULTIES

I cannot say that you have done well in holding meetings that do you more harm than good. In the first place, I hear that when you all come together as a community, there are separate factions among you. When you hold these meetings, it is not the Lord's Supper that you are eating . . . since when the time comes to eat, everyone is in such a hurry to start his own supper that one person goes hungry while another is getting drunk. Surely you have homes for eating and drinking in? Surely you have enough respect for the community of God not to make poor people embarrassed? What am I to say to you? Congratulations? I cannot congratulate you on this (I Cor. 11:17–34).

Four hundred years ago, Rabelais and Erasmus were not very sympathetic as they complained about the ceremonies of the Church, no more than are a number of the faithful today in face of the reforms. It seems that since the time of St. Paul and the early Church of the Corinthians, we have hardly ceased seeking reforms to answer the difficulties of Christian practice.

We now have the opportunity to know a time of renewal firsthand. There perhaps has not been another time in the history of the Church which is such a liturgical golden age as ours. Anyone who doubts this need only read the texts of the Council; they make immense progress forward, and it is irreversible.

It is easy to summarize its benefits: (1) *First place is given to the Word of God.* We still are not sufficiently aware of the incredible fruitfulness of which this Word is capable. We have an inkling of it when we see what this presence of the Word of God has provoked among our Protestant brethren: because of it, the German and English languages have reached their adult age and, among the treasures of our musical patrimony, works like those of Bach and, more recently, the Negro spirituals have been created. If the Word of God is so efficacious on the cultural level, what great spiritual strength it must have! (2) *The place of the language of men is recognized* in its truth and diversity. When we read the texts of the Council, we cannot help thinking of the Book of Revelation and seeing all peoples and races united in cult around the one Son of God, the immolated lamb, without these peoples having lost anything of their unity at the heart of the Church, but having finally become free to express themselves with what is best in their culture. From the East to the West, all sons can share at the table of Abraham, without feeling stripped for the sake of a Mediterranean or Latin culture. (3) We need not mention the inevitable *ecumenical consequences* of these two first benefits.

Therefore, legitimate hope has arisen that perhaps our difficulties will finally be dissolved. But is this the case? These reforms have themselves given rise to disturbances, as much as they did in ancient times in the Church of the

Corinthians. And worst of all, the reforms themselves can serve as alibis to hide the real difficulties. As St. Basil wrote to St. Gregory, it is not by getting out of a big ship to get into a little one that we escape a storm on the sea. The problem is not whether we should change or not, since the Spirit of God proposes that the Church should renew itself to be faithful to the Incarnation. We must not be severe with the changes, but with the motives which push us to refuse them or to applaud them.

A LITURGY OF THE ROSE

A prince possessed a very beautiful diamond, and he was very proud of it. One day, by accident, the precious stone was severely scratched. The prince called in the most capable experts to repair the jewel, but, despite all their efforts, they could not erase the scratch. Finally, a lapidary arrived whose genius had not been equalled. With art and patience, he carved a magnificent rose into the diamond; and he was skillful enough to make the scratch serve as the rose's stem, so that the precious stone appeared more beautiful than it had even before.

Isn't this exactly what Christ has done with our human condition? He has taken our nature with all its dimensions, wounds, and difficulties. But forevermore, we do not have the right to speak of these difficulties as if they were only limitations or worries, because they are charged with new meaning. We are well aware of the narrow bounds of our language, our common life with its fixed patterns and polarities; we must never forget that we betray the best in them when we see only their limitations. In the sacraments, Christ invites us not to cheat anymore with this hope. Our weakness, fatigue, and relationships with others are no longer a hell for us. Our certitude is held in obscurity. But it depends on us that the scratch become the stem of the rose.

During Easter night, the Church invites us to share Adam's vision as he discovered creation, Moses' vision of his people after they had crossed the Red Sea, and the vision of Isaiah's vine-grower after the vintage. A rose is drawn to quiet our vision and to amaze it. Why can't we make Christ's joy ours as he looks at his people on the evening of Easter, and God's joy ours as he looks at all men through his Church?

Aren't the sacraments made to bring us to this joy, even if to reach it they oblige us to pass through thorns of sadness?

Do not men expect of us that the sacraments be not merely the means of a "practice," but the source of a gratuity and liberty which proves to them that we can love human life?

NOTES

1. Erasmus, *Ratio seu methodus compendis* . . . C 113, 5–10. "These good ecclesiastics boast of having fulfilled all their duty when they have mumbled their breviary; and if they have mumbled well, I would really be surprised if any divinity could hear or understand them, since they almost always do not hear or understand themselves when they recite out loud" (*Eloge de la folie,* Bibliothèque de Cluny, 1959, p. 127).

2. *Bypass Christ?* We sometimes get the impression that some "spiritual directors" teach a bypassing of Christ and, even, for union with God, the possibility of bypassing Christ's mediation. In the same way, it is sometimes affirmed, though a bit lightly and without verification, that these spirituals do not have a sense of the liturgy or of the Christian assembly. Before generalizing, we should refer to the documents: cf., for example, for St. John of the Cross and St. Theresa of Avila, the texts cited by R. Hoornaert, "Liturgie ou contemplation," in *Etudes*

carmélitaines, April 1932, pp. 177–215; Lucien-Marie de Saint-Joseph, "Oraison et prière liturgique chez sainte Thérèse d'Avila," in *Carmel,* 2nd trim. 1960, pp. 92–114.

3. The history of religions permits us to see better how, when faith is not addressed to a personal God, it is very difficult to avoid possible devaluations of the mystery of God: God becomes reduced to an abstract idea or an idol (cf. O. Lacombe's analyses, *L'absolu selon le Védanta,* Paris: Paul Geuthner, 1937); and therefore, it helps us to know better what Christ's mediation and our incorporation into him mean for us.

4. "Séminaristes en Algérie," *La Vie spirituelle, Témoins de la prière,* Aug.–Sept. 1960, pp. 153–214. In the same order of ideas, cf. also "La vie religieuse des déportés," in *La Vie spirituelle,* Aug.–Sept. 1945, pp. 142–150; Oct. 1945, pp. 338–343; Nov. 1945, pp. 429–440.

5. *Lettres de Stalingrad,* Ed. Corréa, 1957, pp. 63–64.

6. Cf. P. Congar's account in *Le Concile au jour le jour* (Paris, 1962–1966), 4 vol., *passim,* among others "IVe session," pp. 121 ff.; R. Caporale, *Les hommes du Concile* (Paris, 1965), pp. 121 ff.; and the accounts of the bishops themselves in *L'Esprit nous a rassemblés. Témoignage des évêques au Concile* (Paris: Ed. du Cerf, 1966), for example pp. 202 ff.

7. *Prayer or liturgy.* We regret that this argumentation is so little present in J. and R. Maritain's work, *Liturgie et contemplation,* Desclee de Brouwer, 1959 (*Liturgy and Contemplation,* New York: Kenedy). If some authors' observations raise a problem, we do not think it is one concerning whether the opposition between the demands of prayer and the demands of liturgy is Scholastic or not . . . and whether the remedy will be Scholastic or not. We cannot say, "Liturgy or prayer?", in the name of Scholasticism, because the opposition is not between them, but rather between a wrong way of understanding them which isolates them and a right way which unites them. There are problems that remain: to discern between religion and theological life, to know precisely the different moments in Christ's mediation, and to look for the true criteria of Christian mysticism beyond the often verbose discussions on faith-religion relationships.

8. "Holy Scripture and the liturgy are precious gifts from God to his spouse, the Church. Both are sources of the divine life; both are sen-

sible expressions of the incarnate Logos. But the more indispensable of the two is the liturgy; it is the vital artery of Christ's Mystical Body. The Church can subsist without holy Scripture; and the Church did exist during the first centuries before the Apostles' gospels and epistles were collected together. But the Church cannot exist without the liturgy which brings it its sacramental and sacral life" (I. Herwegen, "L'Ecriture sainte dans la liturgie," in *La Maison-Dieu*, n. 5, p. 7).

9. Cf. especially J. Lecuyer, "L'Assemblee liturgique: Fondements bibliques et patristiques," in *Concilium*, n. 12 (Feb. 1966), pp. 9–22; and O. Cullmann, *La foi et le culte dans l'Eglise primitive*, Neuchâtel-Paris, 1963; K. Hruby, "Eléments de spiritualité juive," in *La Mystique et les mystiques*, Desclée de Brouwer, 1965, pp. 157–254; A. Baumstark, *Liturgie comparée*, Ed. Chevetogne, 1939; L. Bouyer, *Eucharistie*, Desclée, 1966, pp. 21–136.

10. To better grasp the richness of this presence of Christ, cf. L. Sabourin, *Les noms et les titres de Jésus*, Desclee de Brouwer, 1963 (English trans: *The Names and Titles of Jesus*, New York: Macmillan, 1966), and O. Cullmann, *Christologie du Nouveau Testament*, Ed. Delachaux-Niestlé, 1958 (English trans: *Christology of the New Testament*, Maryland: Westminster 1964); I. Hausherr, *Noms du Christ et voies d'oraison*, Rome, 1960; V. Taylor, *The Names of Jesus* (London: MacMillan, 1953); L. Cerfaux, *Le Christ dans la théologie de saint Paul*, Paris, 1954 (English trans: *Christ in the Theology of St. Paul*, New York: Herder and Herder, 1962); F. Gils, *Jesus prophete d'après les évangiles synoptiques*, Louvain, 1957; J. Schmitt, *Jésus ressuscité dans la prédication apostolique*, Paris, 1949.

11. Cf. P. Gerbé, E. Marcus, etc., *Ils demandent le baptême pour leur enfant* (Paris: Ed. du Cerf, 1966); and "Le baptême des petits enfants," *La Semaine Religieuse*, Paris, March 5, 1966; "Enquête sur la mentalité des parents non pratiquants devant le baptême de leur enfant," Document I, *La Semaine religieuse*, March 7, 1965; J. Potel, "Que signifie pour 'eux' le baptême?" in *Paroisse et liturgie*, n. 5 and 6 (Feb. 15, 1964), pp. 465 ff.; *Commentaire du document épiscopal sur la pastorale du baptême des petits enfants*, CNPL, Jan. 1967, special number of *La Maison-Dieu*, "Le baptême des petits enfants," n. 89, 1967.

12. Paul Claudel, *Art poétique*, p. 72. *The spirit is communion.* If religious practice and the liturgy are essentially communion and are

realized in an assembly, nothing should be neglected to understand the ultimate basis of this. What we are outlining here in very simple terms can be said in a much more technical way according to the analyses of Husserl, Heidegger, or Merleau-Ponty. The spirit is "openness to everything else;" and this is the primary truth of experience to which we must always return in order not to reduce the assembly to its purely sociological dimensions. It is true that we return at the same time to each person's fundamental experience of life, the common departure point of every philosophy (whether it be a philosophy of being or a philosophy of the spirit).

Saint Thomas often treats this nature of the human spirit, openness and communion: cf. I, q.14, a.1; *Comment. in Met.*, bk. 12, less. 8; *I Cont. Gent.*, 44; and especially *De verit.*, q.2, a.2.

13. Cf. "Prière et paternité divine," in *La Vie spirituelle.* January 1960: A.-M. Besnard, "Mon Père et votre Père," pp. 5–17; and B. Bro, "Prière ou charité," pp. 18–33.

14. This is the question posed by M.-D. Chenu in *Peuple de Dieu dans le monde,* "Foi vivante," 1966, and in *L'Evangile dans le temps* (Paris, 1964).

15. Cf. Ez. 33:10 (Ez. 18:23); Wis. 11:24; Rom. 11:32; I Tim. 2:4–5; Eph. 2:4–6; II Pet. 3:9; Mt. 8:11; Rev. 7:9; 19:1–6. Cf. the decisive article by E. Boissard, "Note sur l'interprétation du texte: Multi sunt vocati, pauci vero electi," in *Revue thomiste*, 1952, pp. 569–585. Cf. St. Thomas, I, q.23, a.7, and I, p. 63, a.9, ad.1.

9 Beyond Appearances

When we seek help from the sacraments, do we come because we have understood that everything depends finally on the free decision of Someone who loves us? The Christian God is he who intervened in history, who *came before men, who* took the first steps, and who took the initiative for our salvation. "It is all that is good, everything that is perfect, which is given us from above; it comes down from the Father of all lights" (Jas. 1:17). In the sacraments as in the Incarnation, everything depends upon this effectiveness which comes from the heart of God.

The invisible effectiveness of the sacraments is that part of them which is the most precious and the most mysterious. Although it is easy to understand their pedagogical role and their symbolic richness, it is much more difficult to really admit their effectiveness and reality, because it often bewilders us by its poverty. It is not only because they are rich in symbolism that the sacraments give God's life, but because they are the *instruments and acts of God* himself. To be sure, the symbolic action gives salvation; but as marvelous as its pedagogy may be, the salvation it gives is still richer than everything we can express of it. A symbol can never be reduced to what we can say about it. And in the sacraments this is doubly true.

What would remain of the sacraments if they had no symbolic value, or if they were not symbols? We must admit that for some minds, for our sensitive nature, for our routine, perhaps practically nothing would remain.

Let us consider what might happen in a concentration camp. The priest celebrates Mass clandestinely in conditions so dangerous and so unimaginable that some people might be shocked. To those who would be scandalized to see the holy Sacrifice offered in the middle of "mud" in this way, these priests would answer, "Are we scandalized by a Mass celebrated in the middle of the mud of sin, the sin of those who participate? Is our faith so weak that it does not know how to read beyond appearances, even while acknowledging them?"

In these limited conditions, we notice that nothing distinguishes the priest from other men (he seeks, rather, not to be recognized) and that the bread, instead of having the usual, almost immaterial appearance of hosts, is just any poor bread taken from among other loaves, and the wine is just ordinary wine. In such conditions, the sacraments' symbolic extension is exteriorly reduced to almost nothing, although it remains immense in the sense that bread is shared in a place where there is no more sharing. There is no question of looking for ceremony, but only for an affirmation of a salvation still possible for men. To the eyes of faith as to the eyes of love, the sacraments then appear in their most unexplainable depth. Beyond appearances, they propose that we move toward a life and a good which are infinite. In the final count, the symbols are a help admirably adapted to our human, sensitive nature so that it may rise above the level of this treasure; but they change *nothing* in the treasure itself. The reality of the sacraments is given by an absolutely invisible effectiveness, submitted to the decision of God who comes to take hold of our life from within. In this regard,

Saint-Exupéry's words are truer than ever, "We see well only with the heart."

This brings us to insist once again on the absolute difference between the sacraments and magic. In magical practices, effectiveness is obtained by words and recipes that themselves have the power, it is believed, to join a person to God and the essential thing is that the rite be *materially* respected. In the sacraments, everything comes from the goodness of a love that wants to save; and this will to save has charged certain symbolic acts with effectiveness, but without becoming their slave. It is the faith of the believer when it encounters this love, which saves.

This is why, for the Eucharist for example, it is desirable that a correct pedagogy and a lasting fidelity give Christians this spiritual attention which heads them toward the Body and Blood of Christ as he is in himself, because they know by faith that Christ's life is there, and not merely because they feel or have a presentiment of something. We do not, however, necessarily exclude such a presentiment.

Everything we can say about the sacraments depends upon the act of faith by which we know this reality above and beyond the symbols, and upon the act of love by which we are able to appreciate it, above and beyond the joys and consolations which liturgical splendor can bring to human sensitivity.

The thing that is most often lacking for a deep penetration of this truth of the sacraments, is not an intellectual development; we lack the very love which should attach us to being loved and to salvation.

Observe our attitude in the practice of three sacraments which perhaps pose more of a question than the others:

Confession. It is evidently to be desired that the priest's attitude, like the penitent's attitude, symbolize, express, and exploit as much as possible the relationship of reconciled friendship between man and Christ, according to all the riches of this friendship. For this reason, the penitent must pour out his heart as deeply, loyally, and humbly as he can, just as he would towards a loved one whose friendship he has wounded. And the priest must welcome the penitent with the love of Christ himself; he should model himself after the father who welcomed his prodigal son, ready to forget everything. The priest should regard the penitent's avowal more than the content of the avowal, at the same time as he must be careful to discern the exact nature of the evils that have overcome the penitent and the remedies which can cure them. These are pastoral attitudes which concur with the qualities of the administration of the sacrament of Penance.

All this is true, and every Christian must be convinced of it. But if the penitent has the misfortune to come to a priest who is negligent, quick, even awkward or unjust, whose reprimands miss the point of the question, the essential thing is that what the penitent has come for is still given to him; he is invisibly bathed in Christ's blood and purified and healed by the encounter between this blood and his good will.

This certitude should prevent the attitude which we so frequently meet in Christians who stay away from the sacrament of Penance (and therefore from the Eucharist) for a long time "because they do not know how to confess their sins," or "because they have had words with their pastor." They may be able to find more understanding in a psychiatrist; but only their confessor can forgive their sins.

The Eucharist. The man who overcomes appearances with

regard to the sacrament of Penance where they carry the most weight, will more easily overcome them with regard to the Eucharist. We must repeat again that the purpose of the Eucharist is not to offer us a more or less pious state of soul, but to constitute the assembly of the sons of God in giving us the reality of Christ's Body, whatever the state of our sensitivity. We receive the very vitality of the Son of God, the presence of his plan at the heart of our life, his liberty and love, and his gift of the Kingdom. Certainly, we do not want to make communion a cold act; rather, it should be the fruit of an intense desire. But faith leads us to ask for this union with God and the joys it obtains, not by some kind of presentiment which comes from the symbol, but from the reality of Christ's Body invisibly present. The symbol retains its role, which is indispensable. It disposes us to receive this Body of Christ with an attitude in accord with all of our sensitivity. But we do not have the dispositions which the symbol is supposed to evoke in us if we do not understand the symbol itself as pointing toward something other than itself, namely, as pointing toward a reality. As far back as the time of the early Corinthian Church, St. Paul battled so that the faithful come to the Eucharist in order to find not merely the joy of a good meal, but communion in the Body of Christ (I Cor. 10:14–22; 11:17–34).

Anointing of the Sick. This is undoubtedly one of the sacraments where the distance between external appearances and the effectiveness of the act can be best grasped. Here, we are hardly embarrassed by the richness of symbols. In fact, the sensible appearance of the sacrament owes much less to its traditional symbolic value than to the catastrophic affective routine which makes us think of this sacrament as the ante-chamber of death. Instead of reassuring, which is supposed to be its proper effect, it often frightens. And this is normal if we hold only to its symbolism, because this symbolism is not sufficient to counterbalance the funereal appearances which the eventuality of death necessarily implies.

Therefore, the invisible reality must be brought to the forefront, the reality of the power of Christ's blood to heal the soul and body. The man who receives the Anointing of the Sick should believe himself healed in his soul and, with regard to his body, in the principal cause of its evil which is sin.

Whether we want to admit it or not, whether we think of it or not, the soul influences the life of our body. And we should not be surprised at the cures which often occur after the "last sacraments." This does not mean that Anointing of the Sick heals in the same way as a miracle does. No, if it cooperates in healing, it is by an intensifying of our natural vitality whose principle is the soul. Most of us are generally not ready to appear before God; we may think that it is to our spiritual interest to be cured; and it is perhaps to our lack of faith and our tardiness that we should attribute the small number of cures obtained by this sacrament. If it is administered too late, conditions are already such that the sick person can be cured only by a miracle. And we cannot expect the sacrament to provide a miracle. In other words, the effectiveness we are talking about is one which occurs when the sacrament is received earlier and in an atmosphere of fearless faith.

CHRIST'S PRESENCE CONTINUED AMONG US

What did Christ's presence bring when he was physically present? "If only I touch the fringe of his garment, I will be healed." When Christ became incarnate, God had an address in the world: it was Nazareth, Capharnaum, Jerusalem, or Jericho. It was in these towns that his life and actions followed their course. Christ's contemporaries did not make a mistake. Martha's words are explicit: "if you had been here, my brother would not have died" (Jn. 11:21).

When it is a question of a miraculous healing for the body, the effects of God's presence are manifest. Examples are abundant. And so, we can ask ourselves, when it is a question of the spirit and the soul, whether a miracle as extraordinary as healing the body is required and whether spiritual healing is obtained by the same physical presence.

Christ answered this himself when he explicitly and closely associated the two healings. Thus, the evident benefits of his presence for the healing of the body will help us to understand the effectiveness of his presence for healing the soul.

Among the many examples, let us take that of the paralytic: "which of these is easier: to say, 'Your sins are forgiven' or to say, 'Get up and walk'?" (Mk. 2:9). Our Lord certainly intends to instruct us in something here. Let us analyse the episode: (1) Jesus begins by affirming spiritual effectiveness: "your sins are forgiven"; (2) The Scribes sitting around protest to themselves: "he is blaspheming. Who can forgive sins but God?"; (3) Christ answers, and this answer is in the form of a demonstration. In order to show us what happens when he says, "your sins are forgiven," Christ chooses a domain in which we can see what happens. It appears to us to be only words? Then, we will be able to verify the *power* of his word. Christ says the same thing, but in a domain where we can touch the effectiveness of this word with our finger, because, in the spiritual order, it remains invisible; (4) Christ's word is effective: "get up and walk"; (5) In this way, Christ shows that in both cases the process is the same: it is his word and physical contact with this word (he had to be present). And this is what cures.

Thus, everything our Lord accomplishes physically in the Gospel is a permanent parable of what he does spiritually. Christ cures bodies, but always *"so that they may know"* what he can do on the spiritual plane and so that they may believe.

We might reread the following episodes: the sick man at the pool of Bethzatha: "now you are well again, be sure not to sin anymore" (Jn. 5:1–18); the centurion's servant: "go back, then; as you have believed, so let it be done for you" (Mt. 8:5–13); Mary Magdalen: "your faith has saved you; go in peace" (Lk. 7:36–50); the adulteress: "go away, and do not sin anymore" (Jn. 8:2–11).

We might object that Christ sometimes acts from a distance. But, when he does do this, someone is there to ask and hear: "your son is healed. . . ." There is always *human dialogue,* physical and real presence. And from this fact proceeds all the trouble people went to in the Gospel to reach God, even gymnastics, like letting a stretcher down through the roof.

If we have understood this power of Christ over the physically sick, power which is *linked to his presence,* we can perhaps better admit his power over our spiritual sicknesses, a power which acts in exactly the same way by means of the physical presence of his word: your son is cured, your sins are forgiven.

Still, the permanence of Christ's presence among us is difficult to understand. "All authority in heaven and on earth has been given to me. Go, therefore, make disciples of all the nations. . . . And know that I am with you always, even to the end of time" (Mt. 28:18–20). Whatever the abstract way this permanence is explained in theology, we must admit primarily that it proceeds from the practical situation. This was never better expressed than in the account of the young Church: even St. Peter's shadow could cure, to such a point ". . . that the sick were even taken out into the streets and laid on beds and sleeping-mats in the hope that at least the shadow of Peter might fall across some of them as he went past. People even came crowding in from the towns round about Jerusalem, bringing with them their sick and those tormented by unclean spirits, and all of them were cured" (Acts 5:15–16).

We can obtain today exactly what was obtained from Christ in Galilee. This is the sacraments. "Whoever believes in me will perform the same works as I do myself, he will perform even greater works" (Jn. 14:12).

The difficulty is not so much in grasping the mechanism of this effectiveness and of Christ's presence among us which is in any case an invisible mystery, as in understanding its reality and feeling its impact. It is a matter of receiving Christian preaching as a "kerygma," that is, the announcement of a fact that is still present with all of its power for conversion (somewhat as the Pentecostals and other sects want to proclaim Christ's presence to us). We certainly understand that we must expect spiritual and discreet effects from this presence and not a theatrical magic. But we are doing so well at being discreet, that we have ended up not being moved at all—neither on the surface, nor in the depths of ourselves—by the certitude that our Savior is here.

What we find difficult is to have this certitude animate us each time we go to receive Christ's blood in the sacrament of Penance or in the Eucharist. The certitude that something is going to happen which is as decisive as actually meeting

Christ in Palestine. The certitude that our life is going to be invaded in the spiritual order in a way that should shake us as much as if Christ said to us, "Get up and walk."

"Lord, make me able to see, to hear, to walk." "Lord, he whom you love is sick." "Lord, may your will be done." All of these cries have primarily a spiritual significance in conformity with Christ's teaching, but this significance is as real and explosive as would be a physical healing.

We should reread carefully the passages indicated below. They show us Christ's constant will in the Gospel *to be present by means of efficacious actions.* We should pay attention to how in each episode these actions have the value of examples and are addressed to the process of faith. It is as though Christ wanted to accustom his Apostles to the newness of the Christian sacraments even before the quasi-official moment of their institution. And these sacraments assure the living transmission of salvation through the mediation of efficacious acts.

Lk. 17:14: Jesus connects the healing he performs to the fact that the person's act of coming forward is proof of his faith.

Mk. 10:16: "he laid his hands on them and gave them his blessing."

Mk. 8:22–25: Jesus healed a blind man by laying his hands on him twice.

Mk. 5:41: "Jesus, taking the child by the hand . . ."

Mt. 9:29: "then he touched their eyes, saying . . ."

Lk. 22:51: "and touching the man's ear he healed him."

Mk. 7:33: "he put his fingers into the man's ears."

Jn. 9:6–7: "Jesus made a paste with the spittle and put this over the eyes of the blind man . . ."

Mk. 3:10: "all who were afflicted in any way were crowding forward to touch him."

Mt. 14:36: "they took all that were sick to him, begging him just to let them touch the fringe of his cloak."

When we say that Christ baptizes, we are not speaking of the visible ministry . . . but of the hidden grace and the hidden power which is in the Holy Spirit. . . . Christ has not ceased to baptize; he still does it, not by the ministry of his body, but by the invisible power of his majesty. . . . Christ sanctifies, even in a bath of water accompanied by a word, in which we can see only the bodily action of the ministers; it is Christ himself who washes and purifies. Let no one arrogate to himself what is from God (St. Augustine).

What takes place before your eyes is not under man's power; it is he who did it in former times at the last Supper who brings it about again. We are nothing but servants; the one who sanctifies the offerings and transforms them is he (St. John Chrysostom).

We are invited to receive Communion and to go to Confession with some frequency. Actually, God does not want to act with us by pushing us, but by respecting our life's rhythm and law of progress. The sacraments become as daily as any kind of food. But this frequency itself runs the danger of bringing us to no longer recognize the new and creative power of this presence of Christ in the sacraments.

We can go a long time without noticing any kind of appreciable change due to frequent or regular Communion and Confession. But normally, even in the case of Confirmation and Baptism which we receive only once, the sacrament acts like the smallest of seeds inserted into our spiritual organism, in the same way as we inoculate the physical organism with a virus that will benefit it. And the "good" virus should sooner or later produce its effects which are always extraordinarily efficacious. Certainly, the sacraments are sacraments of faith and not medicines; our analogies easily fall under the criticism of someone like Bultmann. But we are all waiting for satisfying formulas to account for the whole of experience.

The person who approaches the reality of Christ's power seriously, undergoes a pressure which he will someday feel forcefully in a magnificent and terrifying way, like a person who exposes himself everyday to dangerous radiation. Again in this domain, and whatever the necessity of theological formulations and options be, it is less a question of understanding what is happening than knowing that something is happening and understanding to what point our concept of life is being modified.

Take the example of a sick person. A person with cancer cannot look at life in the same way when he thinks he will be cured as when he thinks his case is hopeless. Or take the example of someone in love. A man cannot look at the world in the same way when he thinks that love has struck him as when he does not. Something great is going to happen, and this changes everything. And this is the way we should consider the "reality" of the sacraments.

Actually, there are Christians who expect something and there are others who, whatever they say, expect nothing. Those who expect something, do so in regard to the sacraments; otherwise, for the moment they are not really expecting him who should come because he promised to come.

Does this mean that there is nothing for us to do but fold our arms and wait?

Some Gospel texts might seem to suggest this: "then the Kingdom of heaven will be like this: Ten bridesmaids took their lamps and went to meet the bridegroom. Five of them were foolish and five were sensible. . . . The bridegroom was late, and they all grew drowsy and fell asleep" (Mt.

25:1–5). Note that the wise virgins sleep like the foolish ones; the foolish virgins were not reproached for sleeping, but for lack of oil.

If this text is interpreted correctly, like many others that complete it, it shows us that this expectation—which in some ways resembles sleeping—is an intensely positive attitude.

We must believe in him who is coming, and therefore open our eyes in expectation of this light. "The night is almost over, it will be daylight soon. Let us give up all the things we prefer to do under cover of the dark; let us arm ourselves and appear in the light" (Rom. 13:12).

We must at the same time make ourselves ready to receive him who comes: "happy those servants whom the master finds awake when he comes" (Lk. 12:36).

It is not a small thing to welcome and foster this *seed* of another life and to permit it to work in us the rending renewal which is like the pain of childbirth. It is not easy for our eyes, accustomed to darkness, to turn to the light of day, to accustom ourselves to the fresh air of loyalty, purity, justice, magnanimity, and to let penetrate our life the burning oxygen of a love which will enable us to look backwards less and less and not try to find "somewhere to lay our head" (that is, to rest on something else).

Even though this comes about in us by means of an invasion by a power that carries us away, like an irresistible wind against which it is difficult to stand, it will not at all take place without our consent and participation. The mere fact of welcoming our Savior's presence is a consuming activity, because it is a consuming presence. We cannot welcome the fire without having it burn us. This light, this seed, this fire—whatever parable we use—has a name: sacramental grace. Therefore, we will now inquire into the conditions which are necessary for this presence and grace to be effective.

10 *For Truth in the Sacraments*

> Men often take their imagination for their heart;
> and they think that they are converted as soon
> as they think about being converted.
>
> PASCAL.

We often hesitate regarding the sacraments. We are "willing"
—but without knowing why, except for certain generous moments, they bore us. The reason is perhaps that we have not
yet approached the problem directly enough. Perhaps we are
like someone who wants to learn to swim, but who has decided to enter the water only once he has already learned to
swim. Or again, like someone who does not want to drive in
a city until he has gotten used to its traffic.

We learn to practice only by practicing. We come to know
the voice of the person we love only by listening to it.

To use the sacraments correctly, we need to undergo a real
conversion (this is true of every gift coming from God). To
the man who is waiting for us to explain to him what they
are and how he should use them, we must answer: no, there
is no special way of using them and no explanation to
answer the questions we pose, because the questions themselves have to change.

We do not suspect what a sacrament really is. The Curé
d'Ars found a few formulas which come close to their truth:
"we never would have thought to ask God for his own Son.

But what man could not even imagine, God has done." "The priest will not completely understand what he is until he reaches heaven. If we understood it on earth, we would die, not of fright, but of love." To discover what a sacrament is, we must always be ready to listen to it speaking to us, as if it were the first time.

And to be able better to hear this new, unforeseeable, unsuspected reality, we must unceasingly push away the greatest obstacle between us and it: the erroneous and superficial conceptions that we are in danger of forming, and the expectation of attaining clarifications in our false idea itself.

Although we may admit the impossibility of remaining Christian without using the sacraments, there remains the fact that if we look at how people practice them exteriorly we are often abashed by their attitude. We have to admit that Christian practice too frequently covers over either an unacknowledged need for material or somewhat magical assurances or a retreat from even the simplest and most urgent realities of human life. In other words, practice dispenses from other duties!

The person who beholds these compromises so frequently found in practicing Christians can be tempted to have recourse to a more "spiritual" fidelity to conscience and generosity.

We will examine these two attitudes to understand well that they threaten all of us because both have the same origin: fear of the true God.

The most evident false attitude and the one most denounced consists in a somewhat superstitious attachment to the sacraments. Because of a seldom acknowledged automatism that wants to keep God at our beck and call, the Christian may go to the sacraments to reassure himself that everything is in order. In the extreme case, this attitude leads to a kind of Christian magic which tries to control grace and bargain with it at will. The priest then appears to hold the supernatural at his disposition and distribute it for an honest recompense. Blessed medals are as important as absolution, and we are as scandalized by the removal of statues from a church as we would be by the disappearance of the Blessed Sacrament.

This need to assure oneself of the means to eternal life always appears at the beginning of religious life. It is quite natural to seek security in face of what surpasses us: the future, heaven, God. Also, when we possess these means for security, it is logical to attach ourselves to them and to do everything to defend them. But when we take the means for the end, we risk the possibility of missing the end. This explains the struggle between the prophets and priests of the Old Testament. With naive confidence, the priests want to eternalize what should remain provisory. But stopping evolution leads straight to death. And the prophets' role, in the Old Testament as in the history of the Church, is to defend new life; and this is the profound meaning of their opposition to "practice."[1]

In his book, *God and His Image,* Père Barthélemy has described well the inevitable struggle between priests and prophets in the Old Testament. Whoever we are, we must experience this struggle: nothing secondary in religious practice must hinder the coming of the truly new man that we are supposed to become; pious activities must not slow up the maturation of what must be born.

The prophets were sent by God to arouse the heart of his people at a time when the priests of the Temple were in danger of eternalizing the provisory status of the people of

Israel. In the organization of worship, the people of Israel and their priests followed laws inspired by God. The prophets were to attack the organization of this worship and the practices which issued from these laws:

Does this mean that God contradicts in some books what he has laid down in others? . . . . One day, before this ban was put on him, Jeremiah received from God an order to stand at the Temple gate (Jer. 7:4–11). He was to tell all the people of Judah who entered by that gate to prostrate themselves before Yahwoh: "Do not trust in these deceptive words: 'This is the sanctuary of Yahwoh, the sanctuary of Yahwoh, the sanctuary of Yahwoh.' For if you truly amend your ways and your doings, if you truly execute justice one with another, if you do not suppress the alien, the fatherless or the widow, or shed innocent blood in this place, and if you do not go after other gods to your own hurt, then I will let you dwell in this place, in the land that I gave of old to your fathers for ever. Behold, you trust in deceptive words to no avail. Will you steal, murder, commit adultery, swear falsely, burn incense to Baal, and go after other gods that you have not known, and then come and stand before me in this Temple which is called by my name, and say, 'We are delivered!'—only to go on doing all these abominations? Has this Temple, which is called by my name, become a den of robbers in your eyes? Behold, I myself have seen it, says Yahwoh."

Here we have the original context of these words, "Has this Temple, which is called by my name, become a den of robbers?"— words which our Lord would repeat when he drove the traffickers out of the Temple. . . .

What God wants is that the sin of his people may not be hidden by false hopes and false reconciliations. The people must at least be aware of the fact that they are a sinful people and stand in need of the Lord's pardon. Now the Temple and its worship, not as it had been instituted but as it had been lived and prac-

tised, had become merely an easy way of quieting a bad conscience. One could buy "tranquillizers" there for superficial
hearts that had not recovered true peace but an abatement of
remorse through forgetfulness. The sin was not forgiven, but the
need for pardon was momentarily silenced by sacred rites. It is
this that makes the Temple a thing to be abolished, not only for
Jeremiah but for God who speaks to him. . . . And this false
security in the political sphere (the kingdom), as also in the religious sphere (the Temple), must be wrenched away from Israel,
so that Israel may understand that what matters is not the preser-
vation of the idea of merit through substitution but the en-
durance of suffering in child-bearing and in straining after the
realities of the latter days which God is preparing.[2]

No one among us can avoid this struggle. We are told that
God is available to men in the sacraments and prayer, and
that this is a certitude we have definitively obtained because
it is guaranteed by God himself. We are so sure that we have
grasped this fundamental and essential truth, that we risk
forgetting it by turning our attention elsewhere.

In practice, the accent naturally tends to be on the gestures,
rites, and signs which can be seen, and on their obligation.
Their accomplishment tends to become the believer's principal task. And when this happens, we are seeking in these
signs, cut off from faith and used like things rather than signs,
an effectiveness which they no longer have.

When we place all the importance of practice on the external gestures alone, we forget that this effectiveness depends
first of all on the mutual attention between God and the
Christian. The same thing happens here as occurs with children: they give words, gestures, and signs a kind of imaginary
power. Recalling her memories of childhood, the writer,
Colette, relates how she used to watch little insects walking

along. She would forecast good or bad fortune for herself according to whether an ant climbed over a particular twig or a caterpillar crawled off a particular leaf. In this way, she attached little prophecies of joy or sorrow to a chance event exterior to herself.

We must not be too quick to reproach the lukewarmness of our faith or the weakness of our understanding. We must recognize that the conditions of our prayer and our practice favor this tendency to magic.[3] Rather than reproach ourselves, it is better to ascertain this invisible tendency of all religious practice. *Magic is confusion; this confusion prowls after us all the time; in virtue of it the spiritual is treated like the material and the material is treated like the spiritual.*

It takes time and courage to learn to distinguish the physical from the moral, what arises from automatism from what comes from the heart, the real order from the symbolic order. Magic always takes the easier and less demanding way. Thus, it comes to treat an inanimate object as if it had a consciousness; and it tries to win its favor and, in a way, to cope with it. Inversely, magic tries to act on spiritual agents by means of gestures or obscure rites in the hope of automatically unleashing consequences. The Bible itself has left us numerous examples of this tendency to magic: the Israelites, for example, did not harvest a field completely in order not to irritate the spirit of the field (Lev. 19:9–10) and they forbade the sacrifice of an animal and its calf on the same day (Lev. 22:28).

It is honest to recognize that the concrete conditions of practice have lent themselves to this confusion. When the Church says to the faithful, "Recite the invocation to Jesus' name three times, and you will remove a hundred days (or a thousand, or ten thousand) from the time your soul has to

spend in purgatory," it never pretended that this would be
effective by the simple pronunciation of words. The history
of the practice of indulgences has much to teach us.[4] How
can we have a faith lucid enough to see past the sometimes
deformed teaching presented to us and not to think that the
material and quantitative fact of the repetition of the word is
necessary and sufficient to lighten the suffering of a soul in
purgatory? In the same way, this favored a tendency to magic
when it told us we would surely have eternal salvation if we
received Communion nine times on the first Friday of each
month or assured us of a happy death by saying three "Hail
Mary's" each night before going to sleep or that we would receive a plenary indulgence by walking to each of seven basili-
cas in one day, etc.

We notice that in these practices there is always question
of "assuring us" of something which immediately indicates
their self-regarding orientation the minute they become more
or less magic. We are not discussing the legitimacy of the
practice of indulgences; but we do have to admit that they
run the risk of favoring a state of confusion between the gestures and the reality which the gestures represent, and they
prevent us from quitting the childish habit of conferring on
signs a magical quality.

Even granting that, ordinarily, faith is rooted in our human modes of thought, who among us can consider himself
sheltered from the contaminations of magic? Who dares to
pretend that his intentions have always been pure? Who can
boast that he has never placed the signs before faith? The
continuity between the preaching of the prophets and that of
Christ on this point is too significant not to be a great lesson.
How difficult it is to give priority to a contrite heart rather
than to offering of bulls and calves! "Since what I want is

love, not sacrifice; knowledge of God, not holocausts" (Hos. 6:6).

Instead of putting our confidence exclusively in the practice of external works, we can, without admitting it, entertain a kind of scorn for all practice and a secret reticence with regard to simple, direct recourse to the sacraments. They may appear to us as something "added on" which we accept through discipline but with a certain indulgence. The very elevated idea which we have of the spiritual may make us want to avoid every exterior intermediary under the pretext that the only thing that is spiritual and true is what is interior[5] And we know how intransigent this spiritualism can become.

Why does the spiritual man practice at all? He thinks himself delivered because he does not expect from the sacraments a magical effect of salvation independent from the deep movements of his interior life. He has understood that the indulgences do not remove suffering for the man who does not love. He continues to practice the rite well, but because he has to, because that is the way things are done, because he wants to show his respect for the traditions of the Church and not cut himself off from the community. But *on the other hand,* he does his best to develop in himself an "interior" life. In other words, he does not expect to receive from the sacraments the source and nourishment for his life with God, because he thinks that he can put himself in order with "his" God, without their mediation, by the purity of his interior dispositions and the fervor of his generosity and commitment. He asks no more of the sacraments than to keep him in order with the Church.

The spiritual man will come to the point of saying that what he expects from an exterior practice does not have much weight in measuring the Christian value of a life. There results a "broadness of spirit" which, in conversations destined to influence an unbeliever, induces the believer to attach only a secondary importance to the practice of the sacraments. And we hear once again that Christians have recourse to the sacraments only to insert themselves into a communal life, of which cult is merely the privileged manifestation. The implication is that true communal, spiritual, and Christian life begins only outside the sacraments.

And so we find ourselves with two tendencies, the tendency to magic and the tendency to reduce the spiritual solely to an interior attitude exclusive of all practice. This latter tendency looks at everything corporeal and sensible in religion as superfluous and readily doubted. We can ask ourselves whether these two tendencies, one to magic and the other to the "spiritual," do not really have the same root and whether in each case we are not cheating the Incarnation as God has willed it.

When we encounter the tendency of the spirituals who scorn magic, we must proclaim the fact that we do not get rid of a superstitious mentality by declaring it to be without spiritual value. It is not a matter of relegating the practice of the sacraments to second place in order to give the first, according to one's taste, either to a purely spiritual activity or to works of charity or to apostolic commitment. A conversion must take place by which we accept the sacraments as the most precious, *true source of our spontaneity,* that of grace. It goes without saying that this source cannot flow and produce its effects independently of our dispositions and our faith. Therefore, a singular conversion, a singular humility, and a singular daring are necessary to demand from an exterior, physical contact the modification of what is most intimate and free in us.

It is not by distrust that we can cure these wrong attitudes to the sacraments, but by a conversion to the true spirituality of the Incarnation which they propose to us. As we have said, the key to this conversion is the discovery that charity is not in us, and that we need to receive it in the most humiliating and therefore most purifying way, which is the way of an exterior rite. The error which superstitious persons make is to try to obtain salvation from the sacraments without charity and without really giving up their liberty. Love which does not give everything does not give anything.

The "spirituals" make the mistake of proclaiming that charity alone can save us—and this is certainly true—but their mistake is precisely that they do not look for this charity in the sacraments themselves, that is, from God. If they do not commit the error of the superstitious with regard to salvation, whose spiritual, free, and interior nature they understand well—"the Kingdom of God is within you"—in the final count they commit the same error with regard to the sacraments because they do not look for anything real in them.

In both cases, the depths of Christ's Incarnation are misunderstood, not only because they do not want to encounter the incarnate God, but still more because they do not suspect how far our divinization by the Incarnation goes, or perhaps because they are afraid. They are afraid to be made free, afraid of the concrete, incarnate, daily conditions of a personal dialogue with God, afraid to see the light, afraid that it will cost too much to place themselves at the disposition of another. "I am so afraid to come out of myself that I am careful not to pray God that he give me birth. I defer that instant as much as possible, knowing that it must someday come, but at the same time, in the *in pace* [he is speaking here of pseudo-peace] of this enormous, mute fear, my spirit feels itself sighing for the day when it was not yet born."[6]

We never know how far the claims of someone who loves us will extend. The same is true for us before God and before Christ. We prefer to be reassured against his demands of love, and we try to remain masters of it and to eliminate the risks we take on days of special loyalty. We look for alibis.

Despite appearances, it is still fear of the spiritual and its burning reality which animates the "spiritualists," the "apostolics," the "committed," etc.—fear of a real encounter with the living God. Therefore, with regard to the sacraments, they are guilty of the same fault which they denounce in others, the process of the alibi. By this we mean everything a person goes through to try to reassure himself concerning his relationship and his fidelity to God, precisely *to avoid being confronted by him.* And to legitimize our flight, we look for a support, sometimes in spiritual activities, sometimes in religious practices themselves. We stiffen our position to assuage our consciences when we disclaim the common alibi that sees the sacraments as a magical rite, and when we look for a refuge in prayer, religious culture, and study clubs or apostolic groups.

The paradoxical result of such an attitude is that, whether we want it or not, we are brought to receive the sacraments themselves as an alibi. Because we go to them without the conviction which sees them as the source of everything, we finally end up going to them as little as possible and only to keep ourselves "in order."

In this we perhaps find all the errors we can denounce in a practicing Christian: the error of good conscience as well as that of bad conscience—"I am unworthy," "I will begin practicing as soon as my difficulties are resolved"—the illusion according to which one needs to be either pusillanimous or of heroic virtue to be able to approach the sacraments regularly.

All of these errors proceed from the fact that we have not recognized in the sacrament *Jesus Christ himself who presents himself in his body to give us life.* Perhaps we have not accepted this intimate conversation with the living Christ as the center of our Christian life. Life with God makes us afraid, and it is here that, under pretext of the best principles, many find alibis to flee him, just as others have found in the sacraments themselves alibis for the same flight. "How long do you mean to hobble first on one leg then on the other? If Yahweh is God, follow him" (Elias, I Kings 18:21).

A presence always burdens us, and this is especially true of God. No matter how much we know his mercy, most of the time we are more inclined to flee him than to be helped by him; and even while we practice, we more or less neutralize the sacraments.

One of the most radical ways to anesthetize their effectiveness is to come to them as to automatic distributors. "He was able to receive the last sacraments."—"He made his Easter duties."—"I had my child make his first Communion."—"I went to Confession," etc. All of this represents so many formalities, like a certificate of studies or a receipt for having paid one's taxes. We take certain steps, and then it automatically follows that a certain result tranquilizes us or rids us of our uneasiness. So the sacraments are the assured means to avoid anxiety about salvation, about our brothers, and about God.

A very healthy reaction is today bringing us to combat this magical idea of the sacraments and all routine in religious practice. We no longer want practice without real faith, and we are infinitely correct in this.

But from not wanting to fall into magic or into routine, we perhaps risk forgetting just what the exact equilibrium of the Christian attitude is, assessing the effectiveness or the automatism of the sacraments.

At the time of the Council of Trent, opposition to certain Protestant tendencies brought the Church to state precisely that the sacraments act of themselves (*ex opere operato*). By insisting in this way on the entirely particular character of the Christian sacraments, the Church wanted to affirm decisively that *the sacraments give us the reality still more than they make us desire it.* Certainly, they give us the dispositions and prepare us to receive God in salvation; but much more, they realize this conversion that they announce, they give us Christ whom they make us desire. This is why the Council of Trent wanted to cut short any attempt to use the Christian sacraments in the perspective of the Old Testament or pagan sacrifices, that is, as a psychological stimulant. The need we have for stimulants, even in the liturgy, is perhaps a sign that we often remain men of the Old Testament. Those responsible for the liturgy should constantly require the truth: there is no question of entering into a trance together or of looking for consolations; the liturgy is a matter of participating in Christ's saving act in the prayer of the Church.

Rather than beginning by looking for intellectual explanations for this effectiveness of the sacraments, let us try to learn the concrete conditions in which this "automatism" can operate. For this, we must keep two things in mind: the sacrament acts by its own power, but its effect is in direct relation to the expectation and the dispositions it raises up in us. Equilibrium is difficult to maintain. We must insist on the preparation and living dispositions of the Christian, and we must do away with every magical interpretation of the sacraments, and at the same time not give up the certitude that the sacraments have an "automatic" effectiveness.

To enter into the Christian attitude, two points are necessary: we must understand clearly what the sacraments "produce," and also what is meant by the minimum condition demanded by the Church "that an obstacle not be placed" to the power of the sacraments.

We will begin by answering four questions.

If the sacraments procure salvation automatically, isn't this too easy? It is indeed "convenient" in the measure in which, as we mentioned above, if God saves, it is easy to be saved. In this perspective, we must maintain that salvation is not "easy" or "difficult," but impossible to man, whereas it is possible, and therefore easy, to God. If we complain about this facility, we are perhaps guilty of a state of mind of which Christ himself said, "Are you angry with me because I am good?" From some, God demands nothing to give them everything (children who die after their baptism), in order to show that even to those from whom he does demand something, he still gives everything for nothing, including the grace of offering him something: "in crowning our merits, you crown your own gifts" (Preface of the Mass of All Saints, based on a phrase of St. Augustine).

Do the sacraments dispense us from conversion? Salvation is not "easy" in the sense that, by using the sacraments, we would be dispensed from converting ourselves interiorly. Here again, what is impossible to men is possible to God; and the sacraments are precisely God's offer of, and not a dispensation from, a conversion that must ever be proclaimed, not as difficult, but as impossible to man.

What, then, is man's part? Because it is a movement of liberty which God respects, this gift of conversion does not occur without man's consent. This consent is a positive act, a sometimes painful effort to do away with obstacles and every-

thing which opposes the conversion. It is an intense and exhausting work which nevertheless does not exceed in the eyes
of the Church what it calls "not placing an obstacle." The
modesty of this expression runs the risk of misleading us regarding the amplitude of the work awaiting us.

What are the dangers of automatism? We must not underestimate the nobility of those who perceive these dangers, because if they resist what seems to them automatism, it is to
affirm that everything comes from God. But we have to ask
ourselves whether this truth which we want to save from
distressing practices, is not, in the final count, also ruined by
the very way we try to defend it. Those who denounce the
aberations of automatism run the risk of refusing the real facility of God's offer of salvation, and at the same time of
denying that everything comes from God.

Christ's saving acts in the Gospel are eloquent on this subject. It is hard to see how salvation, if proposed by God,
really would not get rid of all difficulties.

Rather than refuse to admit the sacraments' effectiveness,
it seems to us that we should follow God's proposition right
to the end and, to respect it, admit that there is no salvation
except in a cooperation between man and God. If God gives
everything, he gives us, first of all, the power to cooperate in
our salvation, like a being made to his image, free, the source
of its own acts. The sacraments help us to admit this better
and therefore not to refuse what is most precious in both the
Incarnation and human life, namely, that we are simultaneously free and masters of our own destiny and entirely
dependent on God's proposition and encounter in the sacraments.[7]

We often make the mistake of expecting the sacraments to
produce an external result added onto our Christian life. We

are wrong each time we expect *a material result:* for example, for the sacrament of Penance, when we expect a purely administrative forgiveness of sins, analogous to one which would suppress a convict's dossier at the police station.

The sacraments "produce" something much more profound. They produce a modification in the most personal liberty of the subject. What did our Lord tell the adulteress? (and this shows us what the sacrament did in her): "go, and sin no more." The sacraments "produce" a transformation, a disposition, to act according to a new order. "No one comes to me unless my Father attracts him." All of our reflection has been governed by this truth. Charity is not *natural* to us. The sacraments bring God's love, and Christ's love and our brothers' love, to attract us, but freely. Now we must point out where the principal application of this liberty is situated.

Not placing an obstacle is the minimum condition required by the Church for us to truly benefit from the sacraments. But we must now unmask an error which is too often overlooked. When we say that the sacraments act of themselves, automatically, "on the condition that the Christian not place an obstacle in their way," we might easily believe that something negative is meant, and therefore something easy. We forget that "not placing an obstacle" really requires a free commitment and a deliberate initiative on our part. We forget that our very nature, because it is sinful and wounded by sin, is an obstacle. We forget that the divine life and the law of grace encounter another law in us when they try to penetrate by means of the energy of the sacraments, and this is the law of sin "which lives inside our bodies" (Rom. 7:23). The result is that in the final count "not placing an obstacle" is a privilege of holiness. Only the saints offer to grace a terrain without obstacle.

To reach this state, the sacraments bring us to work with all our strength to prepare the ways, to turn over the earth, and to offer to God's seed a well prepared field (cf. Lk. 8: 4–15). The seed works by itself, but it needs to be in good ground. It is an illusion to think that it is easy "not to place an obstacle"; it is the most difficult and painful work there is. Nevertheless, it remains a work of *pure welcome.* Turning over the ground cannot in itself produce a principle of life; fruitfulness comes from the seed. By means of the sacraments, the Kingdom of Heaven grows in us, even when we are sleeping, on condition that during the day we have cultivated our garden well.

As we combat habit and routine, how can we find the correct attitude? Aren't we in danger of telling ourselves that "the work which the sacraments require of us is so serious that it has its own consistency and arises above all from our will. Therefore, let us mobilize our forces and work as if everything depended on us; we can always pray as if everything depended on God. If each one of us is responsible at his post, let us draw the consequences, resolutions, pastoral directives . . . ; let us act, reorganize, and plan. . . ."

Such an attitude, which is quite frequent in each one of us and in many people presently responsible for pastoral action, ends up the exact opposite of what the sacraments demand. If Christian life is entirely defined as a *cooperation,* it is therefore entirely relative to God's gift and no longer has any sense when we say, "Let us work as though grace does not exist."[8] It is as ridiculous and false as plowing up ground and expecting plants to grow without there being any seed to put in it. The working of the ground must be determined and conducted *in relation to* the seed that is to come.

As another comparison, we can repeat that the sacraments'

sanctification is a game played by two, and it cannot be defined without the intervention of the "Other": a mirror cannot reflect light if there is no light to reflect.

Are we sufficiently convinced of the practical truth that the Christian must work intensely to complete what he has *received?* It is a question of very precise activity, entirely specified by fidelity to the visits which we must first of all know how to await, because no one knows when they will occur. This kind of work is not that of a Stoic, because it is not accomplished under the force of rulings or will power. Neither is it an explosive fervor as if there were nothing to be feared. *It is the work of a sentinel who waits for foe and friend.* The Bible continually recalls this attitude.

Beginning to believe and obey the call depends on our dispositions; but after faith has been produced in us, we need the help of the Spirit so that it remain perpetually unshaken and irreversible. Neither God nor the grace of the Spirit prevent our free choice; but they call us and wait for us with patience to come ourselves, voluntarily and freely; then, after our commitment, they help us with all their strength in the combat (St. John Chrysostom).

It is not by receiving the sacraments in a so-called renewed and living way that we will avoid routine. We will avoid it only by believing with all our strength that our first task with regard to the sacraments is to receive, and to receive from a source whose initiative belongs to Another. And it is also in believing that, to be transformed, we must accomplish the task which belongs to us of purifying ourselves. We are soiled. And when we accept the sacraments, we accept a conversion which consists simultaneously in welcoming the enormity of the only one who is Real and in taking all the means for a real purification for this.

We should not be surprised to become intoxicated if, as we put our lips to the cup, we have not understood what is happening. If the fire does not burn, it is not the fire's fault. Fire does not ask the wood to produce its own heat. Christian collaboration does not mean, "Heat yourself, and heaven will heat you." No, the work proper to the wood does not consist in producing its little heat beside the great heat, but in letting itself be truly combustible. It is a work of purification, and not one of fervor.

Fervor, like charity, comes from God alone. The essential has been said. We have shown the sufficiency of the sacraments. But since what distinguishes the works of God is that they exceed mere sufficiency, there is an aspect which we have not shown: the divine largess, far exceeding the requirements of our salvation. He wanted us not only to be healed by Christ, but to become doctors with him; and he wanted to give us the secret sign of this "distinction." It is a sign analogous to the one with which the shepherd marks his flock, but invisible. It is an indelible sign, even if after having been baptized, confirmed, or ordained a priest, the Christian denies his faith.

Remember it is God himself who has anointed us, marking us with his seal and giving us the pledge, the Spirit, that we carry in our hearts (11 Cor. 1:21–22). Do not grieve the Holy Spirit of God who has marked you with his seal for you to be set free when the day comes (Eph. 4:30). (Cf. also Eph. 1:13–14 and II Tim. 1:6.) The rite will serve as a sign on your hand would serve, or a memento on your forehead . . . for Yahweh brought you out of Egypt with a mighty hand (Ex. 13:9–16).

This, exactly, is the "sacramental character": the seal, the distinctive mark of belonging in a special way. In the name of this seal, the Christian is, on one hand, baptized, confirmed, or a priest *forever*—without it ever being necessary for him to receive these sacraments again, even if he has left God's friendship for a time—and, on the other hand, he is capable of performing acts which surpass his person and orient him toward the community of his brothers.

This honor goes far, infinitely far. It assimilates us to Christ not only according to his life, but according to his being; it is a matter of us participating in Christ's dignity and of receiving something of the inexpressible glory of the mystery of the Incarnation. This is because Christ is savior as man and God in person. And it is exactly in this quality that we participate by means of the sacramental "character," and it is to this quality that we owe Christ's permanent presence among us.

We have the honor of guaranteeing the stability of the presence of Christ's powers which we have mentioned:

—the priesthood, in first place, is the distinctive sign of the presence of *all* of Christ's powers;

—Baptism and Confirmation are participations in this power.

Salvation is more important than anything else, but it would be ungrateful not to appreciate the honor which God has given us, the honor he gives our being by bestowing on us the dignity of the Incarnation, and the honor he pays our freedom, enabling us to use such power according to our will.

In this, we can contemplate one of the most inexpressible aspects of the divine *abasement:* "his state was divine, yet he did not cling to his equality with God but emptied himself to assume the condition of a slave, and became as men are"

(Phil. 2:6–7). Once again, in this "economy," God places himself in the hands of men, under the will of men, so that they be collaborators in salvation.

This honor, a kind of bonus, remains subordinate to the essential which is salvation, in whose service the priest, the baptized, and the confirmed must place themselves entirely. Like the Incarnation itself, this honor is given to each one "for our salvation and because of our sins," as the Creed says. A Christian cannot live for himself. His dignity as a Christian hands him over to others. He is another god, but it is for the little ones that he is god, for the lost sheep, for all the sheep. And he should consider himself the most lost of all: savior because he is the first saved, and first saved because he is the first sinner. Every baptized person should be conscious of being more a sinner than others, and more saved than others.

Thus, the Christian is separated from others. God makes him understand more than others the abyss of darkness in which he was in danger of living, to teach him to appreciate more than others the salvation, the precious stone, which he is given. He should tolerate with infinite patience the fact that others can mistake this precious stone. This is the meaning of a salvation which engenders a unique suffering, because it is ignored by too many men. And even this suffering sets the Christian apart. This is the effectiveness of the sacramental character. By it, the Christian learns to love men more than they love themselves, to throw himself into the water for them, without their understanding very well why he does it. The Christian becomes capable of seeing in the heart of every man the temple of the Spirit of God.

This very perception of salvation separates the Christian and also draws him closer to his brothers. God has willed to give us such a taste of why we have been made that it simultaneously separates us from and binds us to sinners. The price of the unknown splendor of salvation prevents the Christian from mixing with human vanity, but he discovers in the heart of every man this same price which is at the source of his love for men, as we love an ungrateful child precisely because of the treasure he wastes and which is nevertheless there.

Every Christian, because he is a priest, is correct to fear "human" ways, because he loves human beauty so much. He is far from men, because he takes them far too seriously for their tastes. They can ignore what is tragic in life, and its infinite splendor. The man who nourishes himself on this too serious splendor runs the risk of appearing to them sometimes like someone no longer belonging to their world. The Christian is certainly separate, "sacred," but it is because he loves others too much, and in order to love them.

The sacraments are like those bad-tasting medicines which a man offers to his brother, perhaps in the middle of his enjoyment, because he is not himself involved in any such enjoyment. He does not join the vanity or the childishness; he even opposes his brother sometimes, because he knows better the seriousness and the value of life and health.

This economy of the sacraments, this way God has of acting, teaches the priest, the baptized, and the confirmed, the divine solicitude toward men. God is delicate in the extreme; he places the power of saving in our hands, at the mercy of our good pleasure. He links the salvation of our brothers to our taking his solicitude seriously. We are free to share in his mercy or not. This power acts only if we will it.

Does this mean that the mediocrity of Christians can endanger the salvation brought by Christ?

It is tempting, and it might even appear more beautiful in

a sense, that this salvation depend on the holiness of the priest and the Christian. But this would be a terribly cruel solution, both for the savior and the saved. We would never escape the dilemma of everything or nothing: either have perfect priests or no one can be saved. This is the way Christains sometimes think of the Church; they cut themselves off from the doctor because the druggist doesn't please them.

Actually, God has placed salvation in the hands of our liberty to give it and receive it, and not in the hands of our holiness. The thing that makes the Church especially hateful in the eyes of some is exactly the thing that saves us, namely, the Mass is always the Mass, and absolution an absolution, whatever be the state of soul of the one who celebrates it. This, because the priest is always free to want to do good for others, whether or not he is in a state of friendship with God. If God asks a lot of him for his own salvation, he asks very little of him for the salvation of others. God's mercy cannot bear that the salvation of others be compromised by the mediocrity of Christians. If there is anywhere an invitation for us to adore mercy, it is here.

In fact, if there is anyone who had the right to be a purist and not tolerate that his salvation be administered unworthily, it is God. And he would not have tolerated it, if he had loved his "honor" more than he loves sinners, or more profoundly, if God's honor had been that of his purity before being that of his mercy. The honor of his mercy is that he wants salvation to be offered to men, even unworthily, rather than not offered at all.

"I will save them in any way at all, but I will save them." After so many Gospel passages, isn't this one of the central intuitions of the Epistle to the Hebrews? If priests are to be creatures of flesh and blood, a choice had to be made between distributing salvation drop by drop by persons as rare as heroes of charity, or distributing it literally by anyone, so long as the latter consents to be "taken out of mankind" for this priestly office. And if this consent is given loyally, the greatest pledge that can be given to the priest himself is that he also will reach holiness across the vicissitudes of his misery.

Every high priest has been taken out of mankind and is appointed to act for men in their relations with God, to offer gifts and sacrifices for sins; and so he can sympathize with those who are ignorant or uncertain because *he too lives in the limitations of weakness.* That is why he has to make sin-offerings for himself as well as for the people. No one takes this honor on himself, but each one is called by God (Heb. 5:1–4).

That we accept God's plan in these dispositions which are infinitely easy on our weakness and infinitely revolting to our pride, is, in the final count, the only condition of our salvation through the sacraments.

NOTES

1. We encounter here contemporary reflection on the opposition between faith and religion. Cf. *Parole et mission,* n. 31, Oct. 1965.

2. D. Barthelemy, *God and His Image* (New York: Sheed & Ward, 1966), pp. 155–158.

3. Cf. the excellent remarks by J.-M. Pohier in *Psychologie et Théologie* (Paris: Ed. du Cerf, 1967), after the analyses by Piaget in *La formation du symbole chez l'enfant* and *La représentation du monde chez l'enfant,* P.U.F., 1947, pp. 118–119 (English trans: *The Child's Conception of the World,* New York: Humanities Press, 1929). We might also refer to the paragraph devoted to magic and superstition in

the pathological conduct of obsessional neurosis by O. Fenichel, *La théorie psychanalytique de la névrose,* Paris, 1935, vol. I, pp. 358–370. (English trans: *The Psychoanalytic Theory of Neurosis,* New York: Norton, 1945).

4. Cf. E. Magnin, "Indulgences," in the *Dictionnaire de théologie catholique,* Paris, 1927, vol. VII, part II, col. 1594–1636.

5. P. Bouyer has analyzed this very well on a number of occasions, especially in *Parole, Eglise et sacrements dans le protestantisme et le catholicisme,* Desclée de Brouwer, 1960, pp. 67 ff. (English trans: *Word, Church, and Sacraments in Protestantism and Catholicism,* New York: Desclée, 1961).

6. Pierre Emmanuel, *Le goût de l'un* (Paris: Ed. du Seuil), p. 183.

7. Cf. B. Carra de Vaux's analysis, *Revenir à Dieu* (Paris: Ed. du Cerf, 1967), on the subject of Protestant reactions to one of the most delicate points of the sacraments, the theory of satisfaction, i.e. compensation after Confession, pp. 270 ff.

Certitude or incertitude: the effectiveness and automatism of the sacramental act. We cite here notes from A.-M. Dubarle: "We can compare prayer and the sacraments. In either case, faith counts on the infallible effectiveness of the human act. But the Bible safeguards God's transcendence and disowns any pretension man may have of disposing of him as he disposes of the forces of the world. This can be obtained in prayer when a man does not pretend to determine precisely how God is going to help him. Faith waits with certainty for God's merciful intervention, but it rejects with horror the idea of 'tempting' God by specifying too exactly what it expects (Judith 8:10–17).

"In the sacrament, this condition is more difficult to realize. The ritual act should have a well-determined effect; this belongs to its essence even as a social institution. But in the Christian sacrament, there are two levels to distinguish: the level of social reality and the level of interior cult in spirit and in truth. These two planes are connected; except in the case of bad disposition on our part, divine grace is given by the valid sacrament. But, on one hand, we never know if we were well disposed (Trent VI, 9; Denz. 802, 824); on the other hand, we do not know in what measure grace was joined to the valid and efficacious rite.

"Beside the social effect, there is a religious effect within the heart

(Trent VII, 7; Denz. 850). Although we know that it is not null, unless this be due to bad disposition on the part of the subject, we never know in what measure it is produced. God's grace is not narrowly measured by the sacrament. On this plane, the law of God's transcendence and man's inability to forsee exactly where religious life will bring him are verified (cf. Heb. 11:8).

"It is absolutely necessary to maintain the distinction between the social effect, infallibly produced by the valid rite (for example, entrance into the believing community, consecration as a liturgical minister, reintegration into the communion of the faithful, the conclusion of marriage) and the interior effect of grace. This effect is connected to the first effect when there is not the obstacle of a poorly disposed subject. *But its measure always remains hidden from us, as well as the way and the time in which it is realized.* Thus, God retains his liberty, and his gift is not totally measured by our dispositions. We do not know our dispositions for sure; we always have reason to fear with regard to them, while never doubting God's mercy (Trent VI, 9; Denz. 802). Furthermore, God gives justification, simultaneously according to the measure of his free Spirit and according to our dispositions (Trent VI, 7; Denz. 799). A twofold cause of obscurity. We cannot even think of escaping this incertitude. Even in sacramental life, God's mystery is not totally taken away. The rite must be extended by an interior piety and a moral practice. This is the great lesson of the prophets, the one to which they unceasingly returned. Dividing the human subject and tolerating a praise of the lips and liturgical gestures different from personal conduct is for them an 'abomination.' Counting on an automatic effectiveness of the sacrifices or other acts of cult to expiate for sins or to obtain divine favor is an illusion, when it is not a conscious hypocrisy. The New Testament repeats these exigencies of truth. The truth is the sincerity which does not betray the ceremonial sign by the conduct and the sentiments of the heart; and there is the exigency for a 'surpassing': the interior sacrifice must go farther and be more universal than the exterior sacrifice. This is why Jesus condemns the Pharisees with the words of Isaiah (29:13): 'This people honors me with their lips, but their heart is far from me' (Mt. 15:8–9-Mk. 7:6–7)."

In short, we can say that good dispositions do not in themselves make the sacraments effective, but bad dispositions make them ineffective.

8. This chronic rebirth of a Pelagian attitude in the Church, that is, of an isolation of man who wants to depend primarily on himself to save himself, is undoubtedly more than a temptation in the pastoral field today. Does not J. Maritain put his finger on a reality when, despite everything which can appear too abstract or too limited in his reflections, he calls our attention to this point (J. Maritain, *Le paysan de la Garonne*, Desclee de Brouwer, 1966; English trans: *The Peasant of the Garonne*, New York: Holt, Rinehart, and Winston, 1968)? "Alas, we'd want to love" (Bernanos). Not only are theological life, evangelical life, liberty, culture, and humanism not opposed in their callings, but none can be complete without the others.

11 Conclusions: The Sacraments and Holiness

Man's desire is without remedy.

ST. THERESA OF AVILA

What is proper to man
is that he himself resolve his problems
and that he know he is doing it.

KARL MARX

My God, if I did not exist,
neither would you exist,
because I am you
with the need you have for me.

ANGELUS SILESIUS

We are tempted to adopt a certain idea of progress in the spiritual life and unconsciously let ourselves be governed by this idea. We imagine this progress as resembling that of architects. As St. Paul has said, the architect first builds the foundation, then the first floor, then the floors above it, then the roof. And we think of the past acts and stages of our life in the same way. We look at Baptism, particularly, as the foundation placed in a definitive way; and once placed, the work is not to be redone, but we are to occupy ourselves with something else. And in this, we feel that we are being

faithful to the language of Scripture. But aren't we misunder-
standing it?

Doesn't such a concept of the Christian life go counter to
what the Church proposes to us in the sacraments?

Whether or not we like change, whether we approach it by
conviction or temperament, it evidently finds us cooperative,
especially when it is proposed to us in the name of progress.
How can we not rejoice at the thought that we are going to
modify things? How can we not look for compensations for
present difficulties by looking forward to progress?

Each one of us is an adolescent who needs to believe that he
is the source of his activities, that he is doing something,
always happy to prove that he is more enlightened than those
who preceded him. Each time there is a break with the past,
we are tempted to think that our predecessors understood
nothing. In 1940 or 1945 for example, everywhere one could
hear "new times," "new era," etc.; everything was "new" or
"liberated." The same is true of our reactions to the history
of the Church, because it is true that every age is a "turning
in history." When he went from the Jewish world to the
Greek world, St. Paul began the first *aggiornamento*. The
thirteenth century saw reason come of age. The fourteenth
saw the blossoming of nationalism and the Renaissance. And
in each missionary stage, whether it be in China, Mexico, or
Africa, change and progress always pose new questions to
the collective consciousness of the Church. We see it now in
this Conciliar and post-Conciliar time. It is not easy to read
clearly the progress of the history of men and the Church;
therefore, we cannot expect it to be any easier in our individual lives.

What does it mean to advance in the spiritual life? The
sacraments offer us a type of progress which consists essentially in ever beginning the same thing again: going to Mass

each Sunday, periodically renewing our confession that we have again committed the same list of the same sins. *In order to live fully and to really respect what Christ and the Church propose to us, can we be content with the idea of progress which is conceived like the plan of an architect?*

In projects which resemble those of an architect, we are not surprised that man needs to progress, because we justify this necessity by the need and obligation to fulfill a program which is made of stages and to follow a plan which should be realized only one part after another. In such a vision of things, the spiritual life would unfold as follows: we would begin, for example, by acquiring faith, and then we would combat gluttony, then we would try to care about others, then to care about things we are responsible for, and finally we would try to cultivate patience during times of sickness, etc. In short, it is a program whose diversity requires that it take time.

But it is not so clear. One day, we begin to feel that these activities are *all, immediately,* demanded of the Christian, and that progress does not consist in accomplishing them one after the other, but in accomplishing them all better and better. And we discover that the secret of this better consists in a very simple disposition called "loving"—and that this places confidence in God, makes us preoccupied with others, makes us patient, etc.—and that, to resolve all problems, even the most complex ones, *God asks of us only one single movement, the very one which will be necessary when we come to die, a simple and indivisible movement which consists in throwing ourselves upon God by faith in the Savior.* We are at first surprised that progress is necessary in such a matter and that we can no longer agree with the architect's idea of progress.

Once we have felt and grasped this movement of conver-

sion, death, and love, we can say that we grasp everything.
And if we do not come to grasp this, we have nothing, at least
nothing which has supernatural value, as St. Augustine would
have said.

This conversion will assuredly bring us to clarify more and
more the problems of our life in the light of the Gospel and,
as Catholic Action says, "to let this light penetrate into every
domain" where it does not penetrate yet.

But we must be careful; we can never repeat often enough
that in the name of good intentions a subterfuge can distract
us here completely from true Christian progress. In spite of
ourselves, we are always menaced by the danger of coming
to believe that the essential thing in progress consists in
passing stages and traversing the greatest distance possible as
we project the light of the Gospel on it. Whether it be a
question of our personal life, an apostolic movement, a parish
or a convent, the error will possibly be the same one.
Whether we have visited an extra sector of the parish or
added one more activity to our occupations is good, but
doesn't God expect another kind of progress from us? The
essence of progress does not reside merely in an extension of
our activities. Because, in the final count, progress would
then be justified and measured *quantitatively*, the sum of the
different social and psychological domains in which we would
"radiate."

The man who wants to measure the progress of his love by
the increase in what he has done for the person he loves, has
succeeded in proving only one thing, namely, that he doesn't
love anymore. The same is true for holiness as for human
love; the important thing is quality and faithfulness to the
first and same movement which gave birth to the new existence.

This can explain for us some of the reactions we find in some of the persons who really knew what holiness is. One day when the Curé d'Ars was asked, "Father, are there any really good men among the clergy?," he answered, "What do you mean, my friend? Of course, there are fine men among us. Heavens, where would we be if there were not? But, to be a saint, you have to be a fool, and to have lost your head. . . . The thing that prevents us priests from being saints is our lack of reflection. We do not enter into ourselves; we do not know what we are doing. God speaks in solitude. I sometimes say to Bishop Devie, 'If you want to convert your diocese, you must make saints of all your priests.' The way to be a good priest is to live like a seminarian. But we cannot always." *Live like a seminarian?* By this we should understand not the illusions or the immaturity of the first years, but an ever renewed faithfulness to the movement of the first call and the first answer.

But then, we say, if the amount of space on which we shed light and the abundance of our actions do not measure our progress, *what then does it mean to progress?*

We are made in such a way that it is necessary for us to repeat even an easy act so that it become still more natural. What is more simple, for example, than "placing ourselves in God's hands?" And then we ask, once we have placed ourselves in God's hands, what remains to be done? Well, we have to begin again, because we are not angels; and having placed ourselves in God's hands once, we do not have the clarity, depth, and detachment required, never to have to begin again.

Progress in the spiritual life can be compared to a diver who repeats the same act indefinitely so that it finally becomes *natural* and not some kind of artificial perfection. It is also like the progress of a paralyzed person who is learning to walk again: the first steps are more deliberate, complicated, and laborious than the simple and natural walking which he will later be able to do because of the repetitions. All of the rational effort and industry we use to organize and conquer the world are orienting us towards a state in which everything will be as calm and uninteresting for the person who likes drama as a walk in the park. "The happy life has no history."

For the person who feels the necessity and nostalgia for attaining such a simplicity, *the sacraments are the indispensable means for repetition and re-education.* In the sacraments, there is never anything to do different from what we have already done. The light broke forth in the darkness; ever as brusquely, but better and better, and in a more and more definitive way, the same light must illumine the same darkness.

And this is the way that so many problems which at the beginning remained "suspended" are resolved little by little —the problem of standing a disagreeable person, abandoning bitterness, knowing how to conduct a certain group-activity, how to divide the time that we should consecrate to prayer, etc. We do not live to resolve these problems; that is not the progress we are seeking. We live for an entirely different progress, that of this movement, always the same, which has brought us from death to life, but which has not yet sufficiently brought me from death to life.

Holiness is nothing else than this passage which, in itself, is accomplished in the wink of an eye, which is already accomplished for us, but which, because of human nature, is *not yet enough.* Therefore, looking for holiness is to look for what we already have. It is not a question of running in every direction to catch whatever star we can. It is simply learning from a first breath how to breathe better.

Every classification of the sacraments depends upon this function. The person who has not admitted the mystery of this breathing, artificial at first and needing to become totally natural—or, more exactly, supernatural—runs the danger of not understanding the role of the sacraments and of not having any interest in them.

If the converted sinner could fully realize what has happened, that is, if he could see what abyss he has come out of, what he was before the gift of God, and who this God is who opens his arms, he would undoubtedly immediately attain the perfection of holiness (and this can perhaps explain why some conversions are disconcerting in their degree of absoluteness). But we know it is a shock we could not stand. Our human nature fears what surpasses it, and this is its misery; but what surpasses it attracts it, and this is its grandeur.

God is above all he-who-has-come-before-us, he who comes. God foresees this attraction and this inevitable fear which are present in every conversion. God answers it by assigning to the sacraments a twofold function: to effect a conversion which is irreversible in itself, but to effect it in such a way as to take account of our frailty and to permit us to approach gradually the degree of love and insight in which everything becomes irreversible. The sacraments have a character which is simultaneously *discontinuous and progressive*.

Each time we receive a sacrament, there is an absolute beginning; and if we have to begin again, it is not because we have gone backwards—though this does occur—but because we are moving forward little by little, from one absolute beginning to the next absolute beginning, until the definitive eruption of eternal life in us. If we want to receive the sacraments and really practice, it is essential to understand that each sacrament we receive begins something absolutely new and that nevertheless we must always begin again.

Something absolutely new which we can desire, demand, and prepare for, but which we can in no way provoke in ourselves and still less replace: a visit from God, a Pentecost, in a word, a birth.

We must always begin again, not because it was poorly done or annulled by our faults, but because we still have to grow more. Here, there is no question of growing progressively from a birth which cannot be renewed, but, in a way, of *growing by successive, ever more frequent births.*

There is a first birth: Baptism. Well received, the sacrament of Penance should be an event as great as Baptism, because the progress of the baptized person does not at all consist in setting himself at a distance from the state of soul of the catechumen who desires the renewal of Baptism; but, on the contrary, it consists in returning to this state ever more strongly and intensely. We might say that the progress of the Christian life consists in feeling ever increasingly the need to be baptized. Penance is nothing but this renewal of the very mystery of Baptism, under another form. It is not an inferior and degraded sacrament, conceded to the weakness of the baptized; it is the answer to the need the Christian feels to be still more profoundly baptized, a need which the Christian normally feels the more he ceases to sin, and not the more he sins. It is true that God uses sins to stir up this desire for rebirth; and this is what is comforting in the economy of the sacrament of Penance: God uses the sins themselves to arouse in man the desire to rediscover still better the absolute beginning he found in Baptism. It is a desire indispensable in every way, when we consider that it is the human condition: it is impossible to progress in any other way than by beginning again still better this entrance into a new life and in consenting to renew the very fact of being born.

Christ said: "unless a man be born again . . . ," and Nicodemus was astonished: "how can a grown man be born? Can he go back into his mother's womb to be born again?" (Jn. 3:4). We do not enter into God's life by Baptism to go out of it, but to be ever more integrated into it. This is the purpose of the sacraments and the true road of spiritual progress.

We are always talking today about the Paschal mystery, and this is good. We have rediscovered to what point it is at the center of the Christian life. But not to remain with words, have we sufficiently understood how this mystery of death and resurrection has reality only in the measure it brings us each day to work a passage from death to life, that is, to "be born again"?

Each time we go to Confession, we begin all over again, and this costs us. Each time that we celebrate the Eucharist, in a way, we are beginning everything again. The Eucharist proposes to us a free and serious decision: that of assimilating God's life and of being assimilated by God to his own life. How can we pretend that we have not begun again, day after day, to receive from Christ himself the strength necessary to consent to it? If each sacrament is like a source of divine pedagogy adapted to our wounded and growing condition, we need this sacrament that, drop by drop, mercifully administers the eternal nourishment which we can bear until we have at last attained our measure.

Everything is given to us each time, all of the divine life and the unlimited energies of the glorious Christ. And at the same time, everything is proportioned, like the bread and the wine, a viaticum proposed for a new stage in the journey.

It is not enough to give us a remedy or nourishment if we do not know how to use it. This is why we receive Someone who begins by reconciling us with our human condition, and who helps us by his light to understand how much it is normal to begin again every day with him. God himself comes to encourage us and to help us to believe that progress is possible. God himself, in every sacrament and especially in the Eucharist, comes to tell us ever again what no man can say and what the Church solemnly proclaims over the baptismal fonts during the Easter Vigil. Henceforth, by means of the sacraments, an "infantia nova," a new childhood, an eternal youth is possible. And when has a like gift ever been offered to man?

Ever to begin again, yes; but if we remain alone, we know very well that it is useless or impossible. With Christ, we learn that it becomes possible. To reveal to us what is at stake in the Eucharist, St. Paul wrote: "Every time you eat this bread and drink this cup, you are proclaiming the death of the Lord" (I Cor. 11:26). And isn't it also our own death that we proclaim, and our own rebirth, from passover to passover, from viaticum to viaticum, until our last Communion? Then, we will no longer need to speak about or to hope for progress in our spiritual life. Our birth will be finished, and God himself will make us understand why we had to begin again so many times.

The veil will not be removed until they turn to the Lord. And we, with our unveiled faces reflecting like mirrors the brightness of the Lord, all grow brighter and brighter as we are turned into the image that we reflect; this is the work of the Lord who is Spirit (II Cor. 3:16–18).